Breaking the Money Taboo

JEAN LYNN, CFP®

Copyright © 2023 Jean Lynn

All rights reserved; no part of this publication may be reproduced, stored in a retrieval system, or transmitted in any form by any means, electronic, mechanical, photocopying, recording, or otherwise without the prior written permission of the publisher. This book may not be lent, resold, hired out, or otherwise disposed of by way of trade in any form of binding or cover other than that in which it is published without the prior writer consent of the publisher.

While every effort has been made to ensure the information in this book is accurate, no liability can be accepted for any loss incurred in any way whatsoever by any person relying solely on the information contained herein.

ISBN: 979-8-39742-305-2

DEDICATION

For Megan Houst
Your bravery in the most uncomfortable situation you can face inspires me.

CONTENTS

	Acknowledgments	i
	Introduction: Yoga Helped Me Become a Better Investor	2
1	Breaking the Money Taboo with Strangers	6
2	A Big Reason You Avoid Investing is Not Your Fault	13
3	Top Reasons Money is a Taboo Topic for Women	25
4	My Money Journey—Spoiler Alert:: It Hasn't Always Been Pretty	45
5	Are You Asking the Wrong Questions About Money?	61
6	Creating Your Vision	74
7	Your Financial Personality	95
8	Becoming Financially Independent	129
9	Breaking the Money Taboo for the Next Generation	158
10	Starting a New Relationship with Money	175

ACKNOWLEDGMENTS

So many people have made this book possible. Thanks to all the people that have supported my efforts. I'm sure I have missed several, but wanted to give thanks to Dana Alsamsam, Lauren Asghari, Gab & Brian Bosche, Marty Brown, Tina Cragg, Kellie Cummings, Marcie Daniel, Patrick Delaney, Lauren Deluca, Heather Dondis, Debbie & Glenn Dreher, Lauren Ferrara, Taneka Francis, Julie Fox, John Galvin, Randy Gardner, Andy Goeller, John Halaby, Jason Hoyle, Dave Kittredge, Judi Knott, Steve Larson, Kris Robertson, Kim Roehl, Megan Rumney, Ken Rutherford, Karen Sheehan, Derek Stubbs, Jill Thompson, Jocelyn Turner-Rolling, Steve Wolf, Barrett Wragg, Lea Wray, Paul Zettl, Jim Zurad, and most especially Jill Farrell and Barbara Hakkio, for giving me a chance to grow. Thanks to Sheila Callahan, ML Fletcher, Michele Giangrande, Taylor Mayo, Erin Sheehan and all the women who challenged me to help women invest. Thanks to all the financial advisors and investors who have provided me with insight and guidance over the years. Special thanks to George Kinder, who opened my eyes to the heart of financial planning.

And on the other side of my world, namaste to Tatiana Anderson, Josh Craddock, Kate Curry, Fred Dolbow, Di Goodman, Ally Hughes-Hetrick, Sarah Kaitz, Joan Livingston, Lynn Matthews, Nicole Mayfield, Paul Malley, Heather McManus Osborne, Duffy Perkins, Alana Roach, Kathleen Schuman, Liz Scollan, Ritz Stasiukiewicz, Jen Swierk, Hannah Topper, Phil Vendemmia and the many other wonderful yoga teachers I've spent time with over the years. And I can't imagine my yoga journey without Catherine Zack and Sam Breschi, you both are an inspiration.

Thanks to my family; my parents, Bettie & Charles Lynn, my extended family, especially Aunt Nadine and Aunt Gladys, my brothers and sisters, Jim & Marion Lynn, Amy Weston, Ty & Carrie Cooper, Sara Lynn and most especially Brook Ondich. I couldn't have done this without each and every one of you.

INTRODCUTION

Yoga Helped Me Become a Better Investor

If the mere mention of money makes you uncomfortable, the discomfort may never truly go away; what we can do instead is learn to work within that discomfort. Yoga, in my life, has been a way to practice being comfortable with the uncomfortable. I'd urge you to begin doing so, too; you can ignore money for periods in your life, but you can't deny the impact your finances have on your present and your future. I am both a practicing yogi and yoga instructor and have spent over twenty years studying yoga. Yoga has changed my life in many ways, one of them being my relationship with money. When I practice yoga, I'm practicing how to be uncomfortable physically. I learn how my body reacts to that discomfort and how my mind reacts. Once you notice how your body reacts to stress in one situation, you start to realize that your body has the same habitual response in any situation.

I realize that comparing yoga to money seems a little crazy. But in my practice of both yoga and investing, I have observed many points of convergence. I am passionate about my yoga practice, and about empowering women to achieve financial independence. If you are questioning where I am going with this, stick with me; I promise I am going to bring this back to money. Yoga is an ancient spiritual and physical practice. To me, yoga is not just about exercise, and it's not just about spirituality. It is the intersection of a practice that is both physical and mental. It provides the opportunity to connect our physical and mental worlds in a time when we are often detached from our physical self, living in a digital world. Yoga helps you focus on the connection between physical movements and your mental thoughts. You can practice what it is like to be uncomfortable physically, and watch what comes up mentally. Then, you apply what you learn on your mat to your life off your mat. For women, money brings up all the uncomfortable things: from concerns that they could lose all their money in the stock market to wondering if it's OK to earn more than their male partners. Practicing yoga can help you sit with that discomfort, which you need to do if you want to stop avoiding money.

The practice of yoga has exploded in the West, in varying different expressions. There are some very influential male yoga teachers, but I've attended thousands of classes in many different studios throughout the country over the years, and the vast majority of teachers I've encountered are women; and, in the classes I've taken, typically 80-90% of the attendees are women. Women possess physical qualities that make practicing yoga easier for them than men. Women are generally more flexible, allowing them to access poses more easily than men. And guess what? Women also possess qualities that make them better investors than men. I'm going to share with you how to use the teachings of yoga to recognize your own strengths and limitations with your finances, to use your natural tendencies to your advantage, and to ultimately get comfortable with the uncomfortable. I won't be teaching you how to do downward dog, or any other asanas for that matter, but I will be using the great teachings within the yogic traditions to help you stop avoiding money matters. Everyone experiences stress and discomfort around money. In fact, money is the number one source of stress for Americans.[i] But I'll teach you how to react differently to that discomfort.

BREAKING THE MONEY TABOO

CHAPTER 1: BREAKING THE MONEY TABOO WITH STRANGERS

Namaste

At the end of a yoga class, my favorite practice is to stop and think about everyone in the room. Yoga classes are fairly safe spaces. Most people want to be there, are intentionally putting themselves in difficult poses in pursuit of something better. At the very least, they walk out of class with a slightly different frame of mind. Most yoga teachers are genuinely trying to help each person in class. It makes me feel good to step outside my head for a second, and think about the good, the light in each person in that room. And as one of my favorite yogis likes to say, the most important thing you can do is to take what you learned from class off your mat, into the less safe space of the real world. Think of this book as your safe space, to explore your relationship with money and take what you learned back into your life. If you have had negative feelings about money in the past, perhaps try and see the potential light that financial independence can provide for yourself, for those whom you love, and for your community.

I used to be the person behind the one-way mirror. I'm not sure what you think I'm talking about, but I'm talking about focus groups. Focus groups are a way to gather consumer research. I've lost track of how many focus groups I've witnessed. A group of strangers are paid to congregate in a room to answer questions and give their opinion on a topic or a brand—whatever the group paying for it is studying. I am a Certified Financial Planner®, and I have worked in the financial industry for over 25 years, studying not only investments, but how people emotionally relate to money.

During a typical focus group, about halfway through introductions (and these are just to warm the group up) most of the participants get this look in their eye, somewhat resembling a caged animal. I imagine them asking themselves: *Why did I agree to do this? This is worse than I imagined. How long do we have before I can get out of here?* And then they wait out their time and dash for the exits as soon as the focus group is over.

But a few years ago, something remarkable happened. I wanted to understand why money was such a taboo topic. We assembled many focus groups in several cities and asked very personal questions about money. We asked them how they communicated (or didn't communicate) with family members about their finances, and to share what happened because of their family money taboos. These focus group participants sat in rooms of strangers and shared stories of shame, betrayal, loss, and difficult lessons they had learned. In city after city, when sharing these intimate stories, people cried.

At the end of these two-hour sessions, something happened that I'd never seen before in all my years of witnessing focus groups. Instead of rushing the exits, people broke the "fourth wall." They turned directly to that one-way mirror I was sitting behind and started talking to the people behind the mirror, to me! What they were seeing was just a mirror and their own reflection, but they wanted to acknowledge the people who had brought them there.

This was unheard of! They thanked us, the anonymous people they couldn't even see, for inviting them to spend two hours spilling money secrets with strangers. And then, many of them exclaimed different variations of—"I've learned why it is so important to talk about this uncomfortable topic…I'm going to go home and have a conversation with my family about money."

To have this happen after one focus group was remarkable, but for people to break that fourth wall, to thank the people behind the one-way mirror multiple times during the course of that research effort was something I haven't forgotten to this day. I realized a few things:

1. Shame and secrecy about money occurs everywhere, at all income and education levels.
2. Women especially have money taboos with friends and even family.
3. Once an individual has a personal experience or hears a personal account of the negative impacts that occur when families don't talk about money, it motivates them to take action.

As women, we've often been taught that money is an impolite subject to discuss. Some women even think money is a source of evil and corruption—that wealth is a bad thing to want. It's no wonder it's the last thing we want to talk or think about!

Listen, I get it. There are many valid reasons why money may not be your favorite topic. For many of us, money is the death of our childhood dreams. After we get out of school, money is the reason we get a soul-crushing, humiliating job. The more the job pays, the more comfortable we are in abandoning the ideals of our youth. Money is the dirty, disgusting modern tool of survival. Money is the pragmatic, ugly reality of existence on this planet. Money is Michael Douglas with greased-back hair snarling, "greed is good." Money places value on the invaluable. It places a value on everything you do and own. Not to mention, the acquisition of power and wealth has historically been a masculine trait. Women's traditional roles—

homemaking, caring for others—weren't perceived to have value in a monetary sense. The act of assigning value to something is essentially a non-caring, hierarchical, judgmental activity, the opposite of all that is deemed feminine.

Yet ironically, the historical role of women is to care and nurture, and an ample amount of money can actually amplify the ability to provide safety and security for you and your loved ones. Money gives you the ability to help others in need. Money gives you the ability to make your own choices. With enough money, no one has power over you. Accumulating wealth gives you more choices in where you live, work, and who surrounds you.

This book provides you with a three-step process for creating a financial plan in service of the life you want. I help you understand your relationship with money, like why perhaps you have avoided making financial decisions in the past, or why money is a taboo topic for you. Everyone makes financial mistakes, but most don't admit it. I'll share all the mistakes I've made, and how I still managed to achieve my financial vision.

Once you understand WHY you've made the choices about money you've made in the past, you can change your relationship with money going forward. As for me? I never dreamed I would have a career focused on money. In my early 20s, I had a terrible relationship with money. I spent money I didn't have on things I didn't really want. I had no idea how to invest. But once I understood why I had a terrible relationship with money, I was able to change. Now I am comfortable, confident, and not stressed about my finances.

Investing is a woman's issue. If you can achieve financial independence, you will have the freedom to make your own choices, live where and with whom you want, and did I say make your own choices? I can't think of a better tool to empower women than to achieve financial independence. And it is easier than you think, especially for your daughters and granddaughters. Let's start breaking this money taboo right now.

Why is it so important for women to talk about money?

Money is the number one source of stress for Americans, regardless of income or wealth level. But for women, the stakes and stressors are even higher. Numerous studies have shown that women value safety and security more than men. And women need to accumulate even more wealth than men to achieve the same level of security.

Why? Simply put, women earn less and live longer than men. Women of color earn even less than women overall. Women take time off of work to care for others, and as result, generally have fewer financial resources than men. But at the same time, women live nearly six years longer than men!

This living longer part is crucial. How many of you know a woman who lost a partner, and at one of the worst times in her life, was completely overwhelmed because she had never been involved in the household finances? When you lose a loved one, the harsh reality is that even if your partner took care of everything for you in the past, suddenly you are responsible for all financial decisions. And some of these decisions need to be made quickly and can have an enormous impact on your future wealth.

In fact, eight out of ten women will be solely responsible for all financial decisions in their household at some point.[ii] But many women, for many very valid reasons, avoid the topic of money. You don't want to think about it, much less talk about it. This book is for you.

Because money absolutely impacts your life in so many ways, I'm going to help you understand why you avoid money, and help you reset your relationship with your finances in a way that works for you.

CHAPTER 2: A BIG REASON YOU AVOID INVESTING IS NOT YOUR FAULT

Adho Mukha Svanasawhat?

When I first started practicing yoga, I'd hear teachers use the Sanskrit names for poses and I would (internally) roll my eyes. Instead of helping me learn, I felt like they were just confusing me, because I had no idea what the gibberish meant!

Some teachers seemed to only want to demonstrate how much they knew, and as result, failed to connect with anyone new to yoga in the room. It drove me nuts! I've realized that yoga and finance have this in common – the use of their own language which shuts anyone unfamiliar with it out. The best yoga teachers recognize their audience and educate rather than confuse their students. The financial industry still has a long way to go in doing the same.

When I graduated college, I fell into the financial industry out of necessity. If I had taken a different path, I know I would have been a woman who hated to talk about money. I would have been ashamed that I didn't know everything I thought I "should" know about investing. Money would have been a constant stressor (it definitely was in my early 20s) and would have played a limiting factor in personal choices.

I lucked out. My job required me to learn how to invest. And I learned it was much simpler than all the convoluted jargon the financial industry churns out to make themselves appear smarter. In fact, the financial industry actively makes investing more complicated than needed. Let me explain why.

When we look at the history of the financial industry, especially the original value the industry brought to individuals, the historical value that financial professionals provided to their clients was information. The New York Stock Exchange was founded in 1792, but participating in the stock market was limited to a small percentage of Americans for a long time. In the 1950s, less than 5% of Americans owned common stock—but since that time, thanks to the introduction of mutual funds, retirement plans through your job, and direct brokerages, a majority of Americans are now invested in the stock market.

Throughout this remarkable growth in the number of Americans investing in the stock market, a key value of financial professionals was providing information on investments you couldn't get anywhere else, as well as making trades (buying and selling) stocks for you. Pre-internet, you typically learned about companies, investments, even historical stock prices through financial professionals. Other than reading the Wall Street Journal, your information on potential investment opportunities was limited.

The value of financial advisors changed with the rise of the internet in the 1990s. Investors could suddenly access a great deal of information about companies that was previously difficult to obtain. With the rise of direct brokerages (think eTrade, Charles Schwab), investors no longer needed a financial advisor to buy and sell their investments.

Unnecessary Complexity

Since that time, many financial companies have struggled to identify how they provide value. An unintended consequence of this "value" crisis was an increasing complexity of the financial content they produce.

Many financial institutions focus on creating content predicting what will happen in the stock market. And since no one can accurately predict what the stock market will do in the short-term, these institutions hide under the protection of complexity. Review any investment firm's "market outlook" and you find dozens, if not hundreds of complex charts, analyzing/comparing/slicing and dicing a plethora (I've always wanted to use that word) of data points in innumerable ways.

To be fair, data about almost anything has evolved and become more complex in recent years. But in the investment world, data points are ever changing. Look at a few annual market outlook pieces from any firm over any period of time and what you won't find is consistency. In my opinion, these market outlooks are more focused on telling a good story rather than sharing consistent vitals.

If you go to the doctor, do your vitals (blood pressure, heart rate, etc.) change with every visit? When you examine market outlooks from different years, you find so many different charts measuring so many different things over so many different time periods. What they are measuring and what time frame they use to measure it all changes in service of the story they are trying to tell. It's the ultimate choose your own ~~adventure~~ chart.

A tremendous amount of intellectual capital and time is spent on market outlooks. All in the name of "understanding" and "explaining" what is happening in the markets. But, at the same time, what is the phrase we hear repeatedly from the financial industry?

No one can predict the markets!

On almost every chart predicting something, you will see this disclosure in extremely small font at the bottom: "past performance is no indication of future results."

Let me say that again—past performance is no indication of future results. If looking at what happened in the past doesn't help us predict the future, why are so many in the industry doing just that?

I go back to the origin of the industry. The value of financial companies and professionals, at their core, was to provide investors with information that wasn't readily available. Yet, the internet has commoditized that core value of information. So, what do these companies do? Add complexity. Disguise the lack of value through an aura of sophisticated analysis. If firms can no longer add value through providing information no one else has, they can make you think these decisions are so complex that you need someone to help you make them…and there is some fear-mongering in there, too.

Now admittedly, there is some hyperbole in my prose. Not all financial companies or individuals should be included in this generalization, and many provide great value, especially for people in specific situations, such as those transitioning to retirement, selling a business, or those focused on preserving wealth.

The financial advisors that provide the greatest value focus on you. They get to know who you are, help you create a vision for your future based on what you value most, and then help you execute on that vision. But, beyond these exceptions, the entire industry is largely obfuscating the simplicity of banking and investing to keep themselves in business and making money, to keep the financial industry, largely run by men, in power while women and marginalized folks continue to struggle in growing their wealth due to intimidation.

The industry is especially bad at explaining things to women
I am a Certified Financial Planner, and often times when I share that with other women I meet, they say something like: "I should learn more about that, but I don't even know where to start, it is a little overwhelming,"…and then they change the subject. If you are a woman who has ever felt she "should" know more about investing, don't be ashamed. This is a financial industry problem, not your problem. The financial industry is TERRIBLE at explaining things! Especially to women, as the industry assumes women and men think about money the same way. This is simply not the case.

And when the industry does provide "financial education," they can't seem to get out of their own convoluted, unnecessarily complex way of explaining things. Here is a great example, that makes absolutely no sense. I'm sure you all have heard this phrase: "make sure you don't put all your eggs in one basket!"

Without alarming easter bunnies and small children everywhere, have we been doing Easter all wrong? The phrase "don't put all your eggs in one basket" was created with good intentions, trying to make the term "diversification" more accessible. But it has the opposite effect, because it has no connection to real life.

Let me ask you something, outside of Easter, when is the last time you put eggs in a basket? You don't, right? Your eggs come in a carton. Are they trying to tell us every time we buy a dozen eggs, we should put them in twelve separate baskets?

If you just take a second and think about this phrase, repeated endlessly by the financial industry, you realize it makes absolutely no sense. No wonder people are confused about investing. There are so many phrases that could convey this concept more effectively. Here are three more coherent, easy ways of explaining the concept of diversification:

- If you were a farmer, you wouldn't grow just one crop, would you?
- Your portfolio should be like your diet—have a balanced variety.
- You need a playbook, not just one play.

The financial industry doesn't understand women

The financial industry is an industry created by men, for men. A great demonstration of that is the "risk tolerance" question, which every investor must answer. If you have ever tried to open an investment account with any financial institution in the United States, invariably you are asked the question: "What is your risk tolerance?"

This is a ridiculous question to ask, because men and women perceive the word "risk" very differently. When men hear the term risk, they often view it in a positive light. Men define risk as "go big or go home." To men, risk evokes the mission every man had for thousands of years—to feed their family and their tribe; to men, risk is necessary for survival.

But when women hear the term risk, we view it as a negative term. To most women, risk is something that you do that is bad, that may or may not result in a negative outcome. Risk is not wearing your seatbelt; to women, risk is not putting your children in a car seat. This is not solely the fault of the financial industry; this question is actually required by the government. The Financial Industry Regulatory Authority (FINRA) requires all financial institutions to determine a client's suitability for an investment before making a recommendation—and specifically requires institutions to determine their client's risk tolerance as part of that process. This is an example of good intentions (making sure an investment is suitable) gone terribly wrong (industry's myopic man-centricity).

As a result of this requirement, we are asking each investor a question which is perceived differently based on your gender! And the answer to this flawed question influences how your money will be invested. One time, when I was presenting to a group of women investors, I was talking about the difference in the meaning of the word risk to men and women. A woman in the audience raised her hand. She first shared that she needed to have a conversation with her financial advisor because of my comments. She remembered when her financial advisor had asked her that question about her risk tolerance a couple years prior. She said, "When he asked me what my risk tolerance was, in my mind, I heard…What is your tolerance for jumping off a cliff?"

I do believe our financial regulatory groups are focused on helping, not harming investors. But at the same time, FINRA is responsible for this risk tolerance question that is not helping women investors. In fact, FINRA is partially responsible for the often-incoherent messaging that comes from the financial industry. Basically, most of the content a financial firm produces goes through a review process by FINRA. Heavy fines can be levied if the firms don't adhere to the numerous FINRA guidelines and required disclosures for content. Unfortunately, FINRA itself is entrenched in the industry norms of jargon and fear-based, CYA messaging. We've all seen financial ads with four sentences and three paragraphs of disclosure in small print. Can we find a balance between adequate disclosure and simple, clear messaging that investors can understand?

The first step is recognizing the jargon used in our industry is unhelpful and leading to unintended consequences. What would happen if we abandoned the requirement to ask investors about their risk tolerance? How would we determine what investments are appropriate?

A discussion on probabilities could be much more helpful than asking about risk tolerance. Unfortunately, there is a reluctance to discuss anything considered "promissory" with regards to future performance of investments. As someone who has written a lot of financial content, I was required to include the phrase, "past performance is no indicator of future results" on many pieces of content.

Rightly so, no one knows what the future can bring. If anyone promises you a "sure thing," you know that can't be true, because there is no such thing as a sure thing. And that is not exclusive to finance, that is a truth in life. None of us have any idea if we even have a tomorrow. But an inability to predict the future should not restrict us from looking at the probability of different outcomes.

What if the industry decided not to focus on risk, but probabilities?
Arguably one of the biggest long-term investments anyone makes is purchasing a home. For those of you who are homeowners, think back to the time when you purchased your first home. Did the real estate agent ask you what your risk tolerance was? Absolutely not! No, they probably asked for your budget and your needs. And, if you are getting a mortgage, the mortgage broker will look at your finances to ensure you have a high probability of being able to afford the house payments.

Obviously, a house is different than an investment in the stock market. A house is a source of daily utility for your life. It provides you and the people you love with shelter. It is something that you can see, touch, and feel, unlike many investments, which we only interact with via numbers on a statement. But make no mistake, a house is also an investment that can go up and down in value.

There are many risks in purchasing a home. You mitigate those risks by analyzing the probabilities, and taking action according to those probabilities. You can mitigate the risk of not being able to afford your monthly payment by following standard ratios of income/debt. You mitigate the risk of damage (like termites) by doing preventative maintenance.

You address the low probabilities of catastrophic events like fires, earthquakes, and storm damage by purchasing insurance. You can address the risk of break-ins by adding home security systems. I could go on and on. And you may not be conscious of doing this, but probability analysis can be personalized for your very specific circumstances, much more so than asking a generic question like, "What is your risk tolerance?"

For example, if you live in Kansas, the probability of your home being destroyed by a hurricane is close to zero, so you don't purchase hurricane insurance, or invest in hurricane shutters. But you do make sure you have a storm cellar, ensuring that your family has a place to go in the event of a tornado, and you do make sure your homeowner's policy covers wind damage.

The same could be true of investing. You don't invest money you need next month in the stock market; you look at your entire financial picture and have assets to address short-term needs in cash or other liquid assets (i.e., an emergency fund). But you also realize the high probability that inflation will reduce the amount of things you can buy with your cash significantly ten, twenty, or thirty years in the future. As a result, you make long-term investments with funds you don't need to access right now. These investments have the potential for long-term growth that will outpace inflation. If you have been confused or overwhelmed by personal finance content before, realize that it is the fault of the financial industry. It's not your fault. And it's going to be easier than you think to become a great investor. You have your gender on your side.

CHAPTER 3: TOP REASONS MONEY IS A TABOO TOPIC FOR WOMEN

Notice what you are holding on to…

Holding a yoga pose for a long time can be uncomfortable. You are in warrior two, your front knee lunging forward, your arms stretched across the horizon, your muscles starting to shake, and your mind is thinking, "get me out of this pose!" And then you hear…

"Notice what you are holding on to, are you clenching your toes?"

Yep, totally scrunched up. Didn't even realize it. Had no idea. Not really helping me with this pose.

"Can you let them go?"

There are so many gender norms when it comes to women and money that unintentionally deter our active participation in our own finances. You may not even be aware that you are holding on to some of these societally imposed mindsets:

- **It is impolite, heck downright rude, to talk about money.**
- **The stock market is just like gambling.**
- **I need to be an expert/know more before I invest.**
- **Money corrupts/is evil.**
- **I can't afford to make a mistake with money.**

Let's try and let go of each of these, one by one.

Myth: It is impolite, heck downright rude, to talk about money

You know why your mom didn't talk to you about investing? Women couldn't make independent financial decisions until about fifty years ago. Throughout the history of the United States, a myriad of limitations put women in a position of economic dependance. In colonial times, most states followed British common law, which required women to give up any property to their husbands upon marriage. In essence, women gave up their legal identities upon marriage, and we see remnants of this approach in the financial system today (more on that later). Married women could not own property separately from their husband or keep any money that she owned or inherited. In the mid to late 1800s, states being changing laws that slowly began to give women some control over some of their property. But even when laws were changed, tradition and social norms discouraged women from claiming these rights, and the courts relentlessly ruled in favor of common law norms protecting the rights of men vs. the new laws. [iii]

According to **Alice Kessler-Harris**, "Up until the 1960s, though many women worked for wages at some point in their lives, especially as young adults, the normal expectation was for women to be unpaid housewives."[iv] It wasn't until the women's rights movement in the 1960s and into the 1970s that significant changes in the financial rights of women occurred. This substantial change allowed women to go from forced dependance to the right to become economically independent. Yes, your math is right: the right of women being able to earn and keep their own wealth is less than fifty years old in the United States. The Equal Credit Opportunity Act of 1974 was the first time that women were guaranteed the right to make independent financial decisions. Less than fifty years ago, women were not guaranteed the right to get a credit card, open an investment account or own property without a man's signature. Women had no ability to make independent financial decisions.

The ability to become financially independent is very new to women, relatively speaking. But the impact of financial independence is profound. Wealth provides choices. You can choose who you live with and where you live. You have a much greater ability to choose your employer. If you are wealthy, it will be easier for you to get the healthcare you need, provide your children with the care and education they need and you will have the resources to leave a partner who is abusing you. In short, wealth enables you not to be dependent on anyone else.

Just over 100 years ago, Susan B. Anthony, Clara Barrow and many other women fought for our right to have a voice outside the home. The women's rights movement in the 1960s gave us the ability to become financially independent for the first time. But the money taboo and gender norms have still limited many women's discussion and participation in creating their own financial independence. The good news is, if you are reading this book, you are already taking steps to become financially independent.

Consider this: what if you went to a party where everyone had to write down their net worth, in permanent marker, on their forehead? The thought of going to that party makes even me uncomfortable. I'm not suggesting you talk to strangers about finances, or share your net worth with your friends, but I encourage you, and all women, to start having more conversations with friends and family about investing.

Many women I meet have a case of the "shoulds" when it comes to talking about investing. There is a shame that keeps them from ever breaching the topic. They lower their voice and shamefully whisper to me,

"I should know more about this…" "It's a little overwhelming" or "I hate thinking about money."

Let's start by debunking the "shoulds"

1. Most schools in America didn't teach investing in the past. We are starting to see some offerings now, but outside of finance majors, most students were never taught how to invest, even in college.
2. Because money is such a taboo topic among women, you likely haven't learned from your friends.
3. Most financial educational content is condescending and judgmental when it comes to money (we've all heard personal finance folks say not to buy lattes or eat avocado toast!) so it's no surprise you aren't interested.
4. Many women have told me they are intimidated to join in when others seem to know so much. Let me tell you a secret: they don't know that much. I can't tell you the number of times I've been "man-splained" to about investing, sometimes even when the man knows I'm in the industry. And the ridiculous, stupid garbage that pours out of their uniformed mouths never ceases to amaze me.

Let go of your "shoulds" and realize just like we have learned so many other things from our friends and family, how we invest should be something we share with each other. Just because we haven't done this in the past, doesn't mean we can't change now.

Myth: The stock market is like gambling.

I often hear women compare investing to gambling. You may be thinking, I don't want to lose all my money on a bet! It's very understandable why many women compare investing to gambling based on how Wall Street is portrayed by Hollywood, and how many men discuss investing in their daily lives like it is a sport.

It's always helpful to think about how human history has shaped us for very different scenarios than we find ourselves currently in today. Don't underestimate the traditional male/female roles and how they impact how men and women approach investing differently.

Many males are striving to be the alpha male. In our power-hungry culture, those who have money or know how to build wealth are seen as powerful. There are a lot of posers out there who attempt to "talk the talk" but in reality, have no idea how to "walk the walk" when it comes to finances. Conversations quickly devolve to boasting, and have no actual grounds in reality. "I just made a killing in 'insert newest investment fad here.'" Perhaps they did, but investment fads are not how you build wealth.

The amount of "amazing opportunities" I've been pitched by men who have no clue how to create wealth, and in reality, are going to lose money on these opportunities, is too numerous to count. But I'm an insider. I speak the language and can easily identify the fakes. If I was an outsider, I would be completely intimidated by these overconfident idiots. I would assume I could never comprehend or understand all these sophisticated strategies.

Investing discussions at cocktail parties quickly become testosterone-fueled environments where, more often than not, the emperor has no clothes. The more certain someone is about an investment, the less they actually know about investing.

The stock market, and any investment, will be impacted by many different factors at many different levels and is impossible to predict in the short-term. Humility is often perceived as weakness when talking about investing, when in reality, it is an investor's greatest strength.

If someone proclaims, "I don't know what is going to happen to ABC stock in the next six months," they are aware of the complexity and variability of investing, they are humble enough to admit it, and are likely disciplined enough to stick with their strategy. The great investor never boasts about their great investment.

The unpredictability and ups and downs of the stock market can make it seem like gambling, but a key difference is there is no "house" when it comes to investing in the market. In gambling, the house always has the better odds. But when you invest, there is no house. I almost hate to use this analogy, as it may seem stereotypical for an audience of women, but I think it's helpful when answering this question specifically.

Investing is like shopping, not like gambling.
When you gamble, you are making a bet on an outcome. You aren't buying anything, as you do when you're shopping. One exception: any "get rich quick," short-term investment scheme is more like gambling than not. If it sounds too good to be true, it probably is.

But investing for the long-term is not like gambling at all. Investing for the long-term is actually buying into something. When you make an investment, you are buying a part of a company. The company issues shares, and you buy shares of the company at a price the market determines. And if you treat investing like purchasing a piece of quality furniture, something you want to last for a long time, you will likely be a successful long-term investor.

A good shopper knows that prices for the things they want are not always the same, sometimes they go up, and sometimes they go down. A good shopper is not fooled by a piece of furniture that is at a really low price but is cheaply made/won't stand the test of time. A good shopper looks for a quality product that is made well. And if that piece of furniture goes on sale, perhaps because the store bought too much inventory, the shopper doesn't think the product is bad, she recognizes a good deal and buys it, because she wants something that will last.

In fact, the most successful long-term investors tend to be great shoppers. They carefully choose to invest in a variety (aka diversified group) of investments they believe will grow over the long-term. They aren't focused on long-shots and they don't make big bets. They don't make decisions based on short-term performance. They are disciplined. Smart investment strategies don't make great cocktail stories, so you rarely hear them discussed at parties. In fact, smart long-term investment strategies are the opposite of gambling, they are pretty boring to talk about.

I often hear women say: "I don't invest in the stock market because I want my money to be safe."

You may be thinking to yourself, even if the market isn't gambling, I don't know how I feel about my money going up and down when in the market.

Why should I even deal with that stress if I'll never lose money by putting it in a savings account? You might think to yourself.

Your balance in your savings account will never go down, but as the price of goods and services go up (otherwise known as inflation) you won't be able to buy as much. Typically, prices go up around 2-3% per year (sometimes much more, sometimes less). If you put your money under your mattress, you are essentially losing money over time as the same dollar's buying power decreases. In order for your money to buy the same amount ten years from now as it does now, you need the value of your balances to grow faster than prices rise.

Myth: I need to be an expert/know more before I invest.

Women tend to think they need all the information before they take action; men tend to jump before they look. We've all heard that men apply for a job when they meet just 60% of the qualifications, while women wait until they have 100% of the qualifications before they apply. Many women tell me they put off investing because they are afraid they will make a mistake. But ironically, the biggest mistake you can make is waiting to start investing.

Women are often rewarded for planning and preparing well in other areas of their life. This is the one area where this tendency doesn't benefit women. There is a huge con to waiting to know everything before you make a financial decision. This is because time is your biggest advantage as an investor. If you follow a long-term approach, more time = more wealth.

The most reliable way to accumulate wealth is to save and invest for long periods of time. Every day, month, or year that you delay starting to save and invest can exponentially limit the amount of wealth you ultimately accumulate.

Time is the true magic elixir of investing.

Want to double your money? There is a mathematical equation that tells you exactly how it is possible. You just need about seven years. If you invest in the stock market for a little over seven years, earning a 10% annual return on your investment (which is the average return of the stock market over long periods of time[v]), your money will double in 7.2 years.[vi]

You may think to yourself, I don't have much money, or there is no way I am going to wait seven years before making a financial decision. Let's look at a very plausible example. If you invested $10,000 at age 21, assuming a 10% annual rate of return, you would have over $1.1 million dollars at age 71. But if you waited to invest that same amount until seven years later at age 28, you would only have roughly half of that, a little over $600,000 at age 71.

The stakes don't seem high when you are just starting out and don't have much money, but you see the biggest jumps in your wealth at the end of your investment career, not at the beginning. Warren Buffet is often praised for his investment prowess and wealth. But did you know that Warren Buffet has obtained over 90% of his wealth after he turned 65?[vii] It is the amount of time in the market, not timing, that grows wealth.

You can afford to make a mistake; you don't have to be an expert. What you can't afford to do is wait. At the same time, investing can be intimidating! But that isn't your fault.

I remember the first time I was given a wine list at a restaurant—multiple pages with lots of categories and choices, that seemed to be in a foreign language. The author wrote the wine list with the assumption that I had the same knowledge they did. I see the same pattern over and over again in content around finances. The authors can't get out of their own way, using foreign words or sometimes familiar words that have a very different meaning in a financial context.

The first thing to recognize is that the problem is with them—not you. In America, there has been minimal focus on financial literacy in our classrooms. On top of that, gender norms often result in little to no discussion among mothers and daughters on the topic of investing. The only way to feel more comfortable and confident investing is to start practicing. You can't magically be an expert to start; it takes practice, as well as giving yourself the grace not to be immediately perfect.

Sometimes after I take a yoga class, the person practicing next to me will say something like, "wow, I couldn't help but notice that you have a great practice." Oftentimes, they mention a pose they are struggling with and tell me I made it look easy. I'm always quick to reply, "you should have seen me fifteen years ago, I was terrible!" Or I share the three-year journey of numerous fails before I was able to stay in my first headstand.

I am not the fittest or the most bendy or strongest yogi, but I've put in the time, day after day, week after week, year after year. Most people can't master their yoga practice in a month or even a year. It takes practice. My amazing teachers helped me begin to understand the complexity and depth of poses that can look deceptively simple. And you make almost imperceptible progress until suddenly, someone compliments your practice. But in your mind, you know how far you still have to go. Whenever someone compliments me, I try to take a moment to feel gratitude for the accomplishment, for how far I have come, for the benefits of over twenty years of dedicated practice.

The secret to yoga is the secret to investing: taking a long-term approach, making a commitment to invest (your time or your money), and recognizing you will have setbacks along the way. Be gentle with yourself if you are having a bad day, or month, or year. Don't expect immediate results. Don't hide from your weaknesses. Challenge the pose you hate (or the money habit you'd like to break) head on.

Myth: Money corrupts/is evil

Maybe I have convinced you that the best time to start investing is today. You don't need to be an expert; you will learn this skill that you have natural gifts for with practice. But the whole thing still leaves a bad taste in your mouth. I'm sure you have heard the saying "money is the root of all evil"—it comes from the Bible. But the actual quote is, "the love of money is the root of all evil." (1 Timothy 6:10)

It's easy to see how one can equate money with corruption. Hollywood constantly portrays investors as male, full of testosterone, greedy and despicable. Think of *Wall Street*, when Gordon Gekko (played by Michael Douglas) famously states that "Greed is good," or Leonardo DiCaprio jumping off the roof into a pool during *The Wolf of Wall Street* (and I could go on, but I won't)—investors are portrayed as the antithesis of heroes.

In the media, we see countless examples of real-life villains, from Bernie Madoff, to Elizabeth Holmes, and now Sam-Bankman-Fried; the financial frauds seem to surround us from all angles! But let's go back to the actual quote…"**the love** of money is root of all evil." The bad actors have one thing in common—greed. And what is fascinating is that, while greed seems directly correlated with money, it can actually cause many people to make bad investment choices.

Money in and of itself isn't good or bad. Money is simply a tool to help you achieve what you want. And if you aren't motivated by greed, money can be a tool to help others: to engage in effective altruism, to help friends, family, your community. Money isn't the villain. Greed is.

Just like women are naturally better at yoga, women are naturally better at investing.

I have witnessed so many casual conversations between men over the years about investing, and a few common themes come up that align to the way many men approach sports. I hear conversations at backyard BBQs, on the golf course, or any other informal situation with men—sports and investments tend to be discussed interchangeably. Often, both are approached as passionate past times.

Now am I suggesting women aren't sports fans, or that they don't have the same passion for their sports teams as men do? Absolutely not! It's just my observation that those sports themes don't carry over to the way women approach investing. Sports are a bonding experience for many men, and there are some core elements of sports fandom that I think unintentionally bleed over into the way men approach investing which I'll break down here.

WINNERS & LOSERS: All sports are tied to very short time frames. There is a winner and loser at the end of each game. It's fun to predict who will win and lose (aka gambling). So often in discussions around investing with men, there is a focus on the short-term. It's fun to predict who the winners and losers (in terms of companies) might be next quarter. Men might be embarrassed, or feel that they're not "winners" with their friends if they push aside short-term investment risk in favor of smart, long-term strategies. They won't be able to participate in these sport-like conversations. In yoga, however, there is no such thing as winning; it is a practice which is best mastered over the long-term, and any comparison to others or racing to a finish line defeats the purpose. Great investors, like yogis, focus on the long-term practice, not how they can win by the end of one class.

THIS IS A MUST WIN FOR OUR TEAM: In sports, the value of your team, or your favorite player is disproportionately tied to their last performance. If a player has a couple of bad weeks, that player could be cut. You can see where I'm going with this—the same goes for investing. There was a recent study that confirmed men trade more than women during times of market turmoil.[viii] This is not a good quality. More frequent traders have been shown to have lower returns than less frequent traders in numerous studies.

HOT NEW PROSPECT: Every year, professional sports leagues conduct a draft. Your fortune as a sports fan could change for years, maybe decades based on drafting the right player. As a Kansas City Chiefs fan, I had spent forty years in sports purgatory, never witnessing the Chiefs get anywhere close to the Super Bowl until the Chiefs drafted Patrick Mahomes. As of 2023, Patrick Mahomes has been a Chief for six years, won two Super Bowls and been to three in that short period of time. In sports, one person can make that big of a difference. Owners are rewarded for making big bets. You see a similar theme with venture capitalists. Venture Capitalism is a male dominated field, over 90% of VCs are men. Venture Capitalists are very wealthy investors who often invest in start-ups. The way they invest requires big bets on firms with limited track records and unknowable prospects. A VC may invest in fifty start-ups, and can afford to lose money on forty-eight if one or two make it big, like Patrick Mahomes. As we talked about, women don't want to take big risks, they aren't swinging for the fences. Another trait of excellent long-term investors.

Unlike most sports, there is no competitive aspect to yoga. In a yoga class, you can't win or lose. In fact, achievement is actively discouraged in yoga, antithesis to the practice itself. If you are striving in yoga, you are not really doing yoga. The practice is focused on being aware of your own limitations, of finding a balance between effort and ease. There are no spectators, and you are often encouraged to close your eyes and focus inward.

Yoga was a practice originally created by men, for men, but recently women have adopted and excelled at the practice. And the same is true about investing. The world of investing, particularly modern financial markets, was created by men, for men.

But several studies have found that women are significantly better investors then men. Women are less likely to be overconfident about their financial decisions and are more likely to consider potential downsides when choosing investment choices. Women often tend to be less active in terms of trading, which is a good thing, as we often see that frequent traders tend to underperform.[ix, x] While men tend to search for the "next hot prospect," women look for consistency.

If women are naturally better at investing, just like women are naturally better at yoga, why aren't there more women investors?

I have spent almost three decades in the financial services industry, and unfortunately, it is still a world dominated by men. In the early part of my career, I would often find myself as the only woman in the room. Only about 15-20% of financial advisors are women, a number that has not substantially changed during the last 30 years.[xi]

I know I risk alienating everyone with the suggestion of combining yoga with money. Pure yoga is done without the desire for financial gain and many in finance ridicule and perceive yoga as soft. But I have spent enough time in both worlds—well, even just in this world called earth—to not believe in absolutes about anything. The world is much more nuanced. Our choices aren't clear; they are complex and muddled and we are much more connected to all ways of thinking than we perceive, even to ways of thinking we despise.

Throughout my life, and with most other lives I encounter, there is an undercurrent of searching for meaning. In some lives, this search is a desperate seeking, while in others it's peacefully aware (at least on the surface). Why do we open our eyes every day and why do we choose every day to do what we are doing? And the less obvious but more important question: why do we spend time on the thoughts we are thinking?

And the somewhat more gauche but infinitely more practical question: **why do we spend or save money on the things we are buying or saving up to buy?**

I think there are elements to draw on from both worlds to help you find your life's path. In the world of finance, we often hear about financial goals or retirement planning. I don't think many women, or people in general, find motivation in "retirement" or are inspired to make changes from a financial plan.

Determining your vision for your life is the foundation for your financial plan. As someone who is approaching fifty and still wandering, I fully concede that most people don't have a clear vision for their life. And even if you start with a clear vision, there are so many factors that will cause you to alter that vision.

This brings me to my practice with yoga, which has taught me that you can have an inkling of vision peppered with plenty of doubt, and if you find a way to create a path, perhaps daily in your life, and open yourself up to a few different destinations, the journey becomes fulfilling in and of itself. But just as important, you can find true motivation to make dramatic changes if you can become inspired in a future vision. I changed my life doing just that.

Now is the time to let go.

Pick a myth that is no longer serving you and let it go. Perhaps you suggest this book for your next book club. Or the next time the market takes a roller coaster ride, notice what habitual thoughts come to mind. Remind yourself that being a boring long-term investor is the opposite of gambling. The biggest mistake you can make is not starting to invest. Even if you aren't an expert. Or if focusing on money just feels "icky" or bad, can you instead focus on the benefits wealth brings to you, your family, and the good you can accomplish with your wealth?

If you have put off investing or making financial decisions, put down this book right now and start.

CHAPTER 4: MY MONEY JOURNEY—SPOILER ALERT, IT HASN'T ALWAYS BEEN PRETTY

If you fall out of a pose, get right back in

Vrikshasana is also known as tree pose. You balance on one foot, and place the bottom of your other foot above or below your knee, so you kinda look like the number four. Your standing leg is the trunk of the tree, and then you raise your arms above your head, like branches. Some days it feels really windy, and your branches sway back and forth, and perhaps you fall out of the pose completely. This happens to me often, and the instructor will say, "if you fall out of the pose, get right back in." There is no shame in falling out of the pose, it happens to everyone at some point.

One of my favorite things to do is speak to a group of women about investing. We all learn from each other. But invariably, after I've finished speaking and the event is winding down, I'll have a woman come up to me and express concern about making a mistake. They may say something like, "I just don't know where to start" or I will hear, "What if I make a mistake?"

Let me tell you something. EVERYONE makes financial mistakes—they just don't talk about them. I'm sharing my own long list of financial mistakes to illustrate that one, there is no shame in financial mistakes. Many of us started living on our own in our twenties with absolutely no education about how to manage our personal finances. It's very understandable that we've made mistakes. Even more importantly, anyone can overcome and thrive financially, despite making financial mistakes.

I grew up feeling like money was the ever-present elephant in the room. It informed almost every decision my family made, with an attitude toward scarcity. Money was more important than me. I perceived those dreaded words, "we can't afford it" that I heard so often as, "you are not worth it." The fact that we lived in a nice neighborhood and my dad had a good job made the extreme vigilance around money even more confusing to me.

So, I became a spender in a family full of savers. I spent as an expression of my self-worth, which quickly got me into credit card debt in my early twenties—the exact opposite of what my parents wanted their children to do with regards to money.

After many years of reflection, I realized my perceptions were just that, perception, rather than reality. My mother grew up in a household full of survivors of the Great Depression. When you look below the surface of the words and actions of my mother's family, the trauma from surviving the Great Depression never left them. It shaped their perception of the world for their entire lives, some would say distorting their view of reality.

All of us have some version of the Great Depression, an event beyond our control that has impacted how we view the world well beyond the true impact of the event. For my generation, Generation X, I think the Challenger explosion, although not talked about much, had an incredible impact.

I still remember January 28, 1986, when my sixth-grade teacher wheeled a TV into our classroom on a cart. Yes, Millennials and Gen Z, TVs were once at least as big as a freezer, and the only way to easily move them was a giant cart. In fact, TVs were being rolled into classrooms across the country, because it was the morning of the Challenger launch. Unlike September 11th, the country doesn't memorialize the Challenger disaster. We rarely talk about what happened that day.

Generation X grew up with the mythology of NASA and a fascination with space (Star Wars, REM's "Man on the Moon" come to mind). We had seen past launches on the news, but the launch of the space shuttle Challenger was different. This was a widely anticipated event in schools because a teacher was going to be on that shuttle. We first heard about the Teacher in Space Project from Ronald Reagan in the fall of 1984. Teachers across the country could apply to become the first civilian in space. After an extensive selection process, it was announced in June of 1985 that Christa McAuliffe was chosen. Imagine that: it was not a billionaire, but a humble high school social studies teacher going to space. That fall, teachers across the country used the Teachers in Space Project as a real-life science lesson, with lectures, experiments, even stuff exploding, all leading up to the launch day in January. Christa was planning to teach lessons live from space, with the first lesson called "The Ultimate Field Trip."

At that point in time, it was rare to have a TV in the classroom, the only computers were in a lab, and no one had a mobile phone. Our teachers had spent the entire fall term generating excitement for this special day, when one of their very own was to accomplish something no other civilian had before. But in one of the first collective tragedies broadcast and experienced live and simultaneously before our entire nation, giddiness turned abruptly to shock and horror. Children who, moments before, had chanted in unison the countdown to blast off "3…2…1…" in anticipation of cheering the liftoff, became silent. We will never forget that plume of smoke dividing into a "v" shaped cloud, representing a day gone terribly wrong.

This was not an act of violence, like the Kennedy assassination or 9/11, but a failure of our own making. As with most failures, it became tucked away in the corner of our memories, which is often easier than reliving it time and time again. The impact of this event has been largely unexamined, just like Generation X is largely overlooked. But Generation X is now beginning to peak in terms of their control of power and wealth, and it is worth understanding how the impact of one of their formative collective experiences makes them very different than other generations. Collective tragedy displayed live on TV is unfortunately commonplace now, but in 1986, it was an unwitting experiment in trauma for a generation.

And, as always, with every generalization there are exceptions, but you can see the fallout from that day in Generation X's distrust of institutions, pessimist outlook, angst, expectation of always falling short, understanding that nothing is certain, and resignation when things do go wrong. Nearly half of Gen Xers don't believe they will receive ANY Social Security benefits.[xii] Despite having paid into the program thousands and thousands of dollars, most don't think they will get a single penny. This is because Gen Xers have experienced promises broken by the government before—vividly, right before their eyes. See how that childhood experience influenced an expectation tied to finances?

Generation X had been training for the global pandemic their entire lives. And in my field of financial planning, Generation X will define and approach retirement, financial markets and their legacy in a radically different way than prior generations. And if you still have doubt that the events of one day can leave an indelible impression on a generation, ponder the thought that after thirty plus years of Americans turning their attention away from the space program, two members of Generation X, Jeff Besos and Elon Musk, are seeking to break barriers in space once again.

I know I've carried on way too long about this one event, but my hope is to illustrate how one day can shape a generation. Just as Millennials grew up under the shadow of 9/11, just like my mother grew up under the shadow of the Great Depression—each of these generational experiences and traumas leave an indelible stain on our beliefs about money.

Let's get back to my mother. She was determined to save and make choices to ensure I would never feel anything like the things her family experienced in the Great Depression, not even close. What a gift that was! But as a child, I took it differently. And that so often happens with money.

Our attitudes and beliefs about money are uniquely our own, based on our own experiences.

Far too often, we can't understand why those closest to us can have such different attitudes and beliefs, and then we make assumptions that cause us and the person we love pain. My mom was trying to teach me the importance of saving, but my immature brain made it about my immediate gratification, and then decided I was unloved because she wouldn't give in to my spending impulses. At least I eventually figured it out.

My 20s started off on very shaky financial ground.
I spent a lot of time in my early twenties just surviving financially, living paycheck to paycheck. When you don't have enough money to pay your bills, money can become all consuming. You can't think about investing and long-term financial goals if you are uncertain if you have enough money to buy groceries. You can only focus on getting by until your next paycheck.

I get so annoyed at the self-righteous, out-of-touch "financial education" the industry puts out about how much money you could save for retirement if you just "skipped buying lattes." I know when I was just starting out, lattes were not in my universe; I felt lucky if I had $10 to put in my gas tank. I remember the day before my paycheck, if I was out of money, I would go the grocery store, get some food, and write a check for $20 over, just so I could have some cash, knowing that the check wouldn't clear until my paycheck hit my account. I was always behind, and as a result, my credit card debt bloomed. I felt like such an idiot, I had just gotten my first job working in the financial industry, learning all about investing and creating wealth. But I was doing the exact opposite of what I was learning; I was creating credit card debt instead of wealth.

I didn't want to discuss it with anyone. I was ashamed on the inside, fiercely independent on the outside. I didn't want to ask anyone for help. I was going to fix it by myself. The daily stress of knowing that I owed money, and not knowing when I would be able to pay it off motivated me to figure out what I could do differently. Eventually, I realized the steps I needed to take to change my situation. I cut my expenses, went back to having a roommate, restructured my credit card debt and finally paid it off.

The experience of racking up credit card debt and then painfully paying it off made me start to examine my relationship with money. I realized that I was spending money as an expression of my self-worth. I wanted to look successful, so I bought clothes and shoes I couldn't afford. If I saw something I wanted, I told myself I was worth it! I justified it by telling myself I would pay it off with my bonus, which, by the way, wasn't coming until months later. At my job, I was learning about the importance of having an emergency fund and investing for my future, so I felt like a complete fraud. But at least I didn't look like one.

How we treat our money aligns with our own life experience and personal maturity. There have been many stories of famous actors, athletes and entertainers who made a ton of money at a very young age, and then lost it all. I think many individuals in their early 20s have gotten their first job and found themselves overspending, albeit on a much smaller scale than the prodigies who find themselves incredibly wealthy yet still too immature to use their wealth appropriately. As we get older, life intercedes, and often growing responsibilities and growing families cause individuals to reassess what they value and change their money habits. Despite all of the financial mistakes I made in my early twenties, the one thing I did right was pay myself first. I started saving for my retirement from my first paycheck at my first job after college, even while having credit card debt. Time, as I've suggested, is an investor's biggest advantage.

Another Colossal Financial Mistake

In my early thirties, my primary financial goal was to buy my first home. I had spent my twenties watching friends who had bought homes gain wealth through increasing home values. I had recently gotten married, so my perception of buying a home of our own wasn't just about money; it could help us reach certain goals, could be a place that my husband at the time could start his business. Even though I knew that housing prices had gone up and up and up, and that all markets are cyclical, I didn't want my life to be on hold any longer.

When the housing market dipped a little on the east coast where I was living, I thought I was being savvy—*now is the time to buy,* I convinced myself. So, I bought my first house in 2007, just before the 2008 global financial crisis, and this unfortunate choice impacted my life for several years. As we quickly became underwater in our home (meaning the amount we owed was more than we could get by selling it), I felt trapped. Trapped in the house, trapped in my job, trapped in my marriage. Whether I liked it or not, I was stuck. Ironically, the urge to get "unstuck" and move forward with achieving my financial goal of buying my first home actually resulted in me feeling even more stuck than before.

I was stuck in that house for a few years, and my time owning that house outlasted my time being married, which brought me to yet another financial pickle. I was getting divorced and wasn't quite sure how I would pay for the divorce. I had made and saved significantly more than my ex, and as a result, would have to pay him a very large settlement. I didn't want to sell the house we had bought in 2007 as it was still undervalued, but at the same time, wanted to minimize any withdrawals from my retirement fund, even though its value was one of the driving forces of the settlement. And oh, by the way, I was also still supporting my ex-spouse for the year we had to live apart before the divorce (according to state law). I also had to pay the fees of first a mediator, then both attorneys, and one more new financial burden: alimony.

Yes, the hard-fought financial equality provisions I talked about earlier cut both ways; if you are the spouse making more money, in some states you are going to have to pay alimony to your partner, regardless of your gender. I was facing a hefty monthly alimony payment for the next few years, and without the cash flow to do it with my current income. I knew I wasn't going to go into debt again, so I had to find another way. Especially because most couples end up selling the house and using the equity to help settle a divorce. Our house had not yet regained the value it had lost during the financial crisis, even seven years later when our divorce was finalized.

Luckily, I had learned a lot more about finances at this point. I understood the biggest potential financial pitfalls of divorce and was determined to minimize the impact on my finances. I'll be damned if I was going to sell my first house, the one that I scrimped and saved for a down payment, the one that I thought of as a long-term investment, the one that I didn't even particularly like but settled for because it fit our needs at the time, the one that we had to invest even more money in after we uncovered a shoddy bathroom update, the one that I drove two hours to a rock quarry to pick out a unique, perfect slab of granite for the new, beautiful kitchen, I was not going to sell THAT house at a loss. Ok, rant over.

There were also some rational reasons for my reluctance to sell. Seven years after the global financial crisis, the economy was picking up. The housing market was recovering, and all signs pointed to significant price increases in our area in just a few years, as new building had come to a halt and an increase in demand was imminent.

I was NOT going to make another real estate timing mistake. The financial situation I was in was a temporary cash flow issue. If I could solve the temporary issue, the investment in my first house would pay off. All I needed to do was increase my cash flow for the next few years. My divorce inadvertently became my first entry into the world of entrepreneurship. I created an in-law suite with a separate entrance into part of the house I wasn't using and got into the short-term rental business.

I was in the right place at the right time. I was terrified but determined to make this work. A great location coupled with my marketing skills and understanding of customer experience helped me become a great host. I was always thinking of ways I could make my guests stay better. One of my first guests was a valuable learning experience. A young couple checked in, and shortly after messaged me that the electricity had gone out. I was jammed at work, over an hour away, and with no discernible ability to restore power to the house (after confirming it wasn't impacting the entire neighborhood), I told them my "handyman" would be right over to fix the problem. Then I called a friend and begged for help. I knew he was handy, and he quickly realized a fuse had blown, problem solved! But I knew a power outage on day one of their stay wasn't great, and I desperately needed good reviews for this new property. After apologizing profusely, I proactively refunded the guest that night of their stay. Because shit happens. You can't control that. But you can control how you respond, and I was determined to change this bad experience into a remarkably good one for this guest. I wanted to do something that would make them say to their friends after the stay, "we had an issue, but the host made sure to make it right, and then some." And sure enough, I got a glowing review from that guest. I'm not suggesting that a refund is an appropriate response for every guest, but I knew how important positive early reviews would be. And my first business had amazing cash flow for several years, until COVID hit. But by then, I just realized I had a new challenge and needed to adapt once again. And I'm proud to say that I sold that house at a great price well above what I initially paid for, even above asking price, when the time was right! With any long-term investment, having the patience to ride out price dips was a lesson I had learned and applied.

    This experience also made me recognize the value of an investment that provides ongoing cash flow, in addition to the potential for long-term growth. A common investment that provides ongoing cash flow is a rental property. Often these are called "passive investments," but in reality, owning a rental property requires ongoing management. Investing in real estate has its own trade-offs to consider, but a source of ongoing cash flow that appreciates can be a fantastic opportunity on the path to financial freedom.

After my divorce, I began to take a hard look at the life I had created. As I reflected on my big life choices to date, I realized that many of my choices had been influenced by my own financial myths. One example was my career. I had spent my entire career as an employee of a large corporation. Once I decided to get honest with myself, I realized I was settling for something I didn't truly love because of my own financial fears. I had never thought of becoming an entrepreneur–that seemed too risky. But when I started my own side-hustle out of necessity, it didn't feel like working, I loved the experience! I realized I had the competence and perseverance to be successful on my own. Even if starting my own business felt terrifying. After spending years feeling stuck, in large part, because of financial decisions I had made, I decided I didn't want to waste any more time. I wasn't going to continue to sacrifice my current existence to wait for "retirement," I wanted to start living the life I wanted now, based on what was truly important to me. After time and reflection, I created a new vision for my life which included a specific purpose. The unexamined beliefs I had about money hadn't served me. Once I had identified them, I could let them go. This is my purpose going forward, to help people better understand their relationship with money. And I want to break the money taboo among women, which I believe will help women become financially independent. My vision for my life was to live in a small community in a place of natural beauty that I adored and had been visiting for over twenty years: St. John, in the Virgin Islands. I hung a picture of the island of St. John in my office to remind me every day of my vision. Gradually, I found less and less pleasure in buying things, as I realized every new purchase was just delaying my vision. The pandemic gave me an even greater sense of urgency to find a way to live the life I wanted now. My vision served as a guidepost for my financial decisions, would a decision get me closer or further away to achieving my vision?

My vision helped me focus on what was important to me. Your vision is what you want your life, not your retirement, to look like. Your financial plan should be focused on helping you achieve your vision as soon as possible. But you can't have one without the other.

In the coming chapters I'm going to help you create your vision and your financial plan to help you live the life you want as soon as you possibly can. My life has completely changed because I took the time to decide what I wanted my life to look like. I highly recommend it – once you create your vision, you will wonder why you didn't do it sooner.

Financial mistakes happen. A financially independent life is created. Don't let your fear of making financial mistakes delay the creation of your financially independent life. Let me assure you of one thing. You will make financial mistakes. The more you can understand WHY you made those mistakes, the more you will be able to avoid making similar mistakes in the future, and understanding your financial personality is the first step to understanding why you have made past financial mistakes. We'll cover financial personalities later, but the first, and most important thing you can do to secure your financial independence is to create a vision of your ideal life. Our wealth is not in service of our wealth. Our wealth is in service of our vision for our ideal life.

CHAPTER 5: ARE YOU ASKING THE WRONG QUESTIONS ABOUT MONEY?

Come back to your breath

The act of breathing is fascinating. Besides your heart beating, taking a breath is an activity you are going to do more frequently than anything else in your lifetime. Assuming you live a normal life expectancy, you are going to breathe nearly 700 million times in your life. Let me say that again, you will take close to 700 million breaths. Unlike your heart beating, you have the ability to consciously control your breathing, slow it down, or speed it up. For many years, I was largely unaware of my breath. But during my years of practicing yoga, I would hear teachers say "come back to your breath" over and over and over again. I gradually realized that being aware of your breath was the most important part of the practice, not the pose. Slowing down your breathing turns off your fight-or-flight reflex and decreases your stress. When you watch your breath, it naturally signals you to slow down when you are pushing too hard. The practice of coming back to your breath gives you a center for your practice, a moment to notice how you are reacting, physically and mentally, to discomfort. It gives you the space to intentionally choose how you respond. Coming back to my breath has helped me tremendously off my mat as well. Before I give a speech, I take four slow, deep breaths. It immediately calms me down and helps me focus before I go onstage. Having a financial vision that you can focus on and return to has the equivalent benefits in life that "coming back to the breath" has in yoga.

"Should I invest in cryptocurrency?"

"Do you think a Roth IRA is the way to go?"

"Thing have been so crazy lately, what do you think is going to happen to the market?"

These are just a sample of questions I typically get from people I've just met, when they find out I am a Certified Financial Planner. Most people ask questions that are difficult, if not impossible to answer without knowing the answers to several other questions about their lives and specific financial situation, not to mention their personal attitudes and beliefs about money.

The questions above assume a couple things.

1. You know exactly what you are investing FOR
2. You will make an optimal, rational decision once you get your question answered.

Knowledge is important, but it isn't enough. There are three steps to achieving financial independence, which I'll break down for you here.

Step 1: Identifying your financial vision. Answering this question in detail:

Why are you saving and investing?

MOST PEOPLE SKIP THIS STEP

Step 2: Creating a strategy to achieve your vision and become financially independent.

This is the easy part, and the focus of a lot of questions I receive. But Step 2 will never be effective without Step 1 and 3.

Step 3: Executing on your strategy.

THIS IS WHERE MANY PEOPLE GET DERAILED

Executing on your strategy to achieve your vision and become financially independent involves changing the choices you make every day involving money. You can "know" how to lose weight, but there are lot of factors that can impact your ability to change and achieve the results you want.

Each of these three steps require different skills, and different people will have a natural talent or affinity for one of the three steps.

Most of the content around investing focuses on step two, creating a strategy, with a focus on the financial independence part, aka…how can I make us much money as I can, as quickly as I can. You can accumulate vast amounts of wealth and still have a miserable existence. We've all seen a multitude of celebrities who have all the money and none of the life they want. That is why Step 1 is so important. Creating your vision for your life is a life-long pursuit. One that many defer until…

…*Retirement: "I'll figure out what I want to do when I retire."*

…*I have enough money: "I can't even start to think about what I want to do until I pay off that loan."*

…*The kids are grown: "I don't have time to think about my vision for my life, I'm too busy!"*

…*Or insert your own personal procrastination excuse here:*

Come back to the breath. It all starts and ends with your vision. You can't have a successful investment strategy without knowing what you are saving and investing for.

Why should you create a vision?

Let's start to create your vision for your life. And if this already makes the muscles in your jaw clench up slightly, don't worry. Your vision isn't permanent; in fact, it will change over time. But if you don't have a vision, you may find yourself spending years doing things you didn't intend to do, because you never determined what you wanted to do with your time.

There was an academic study done that looked at financial decision-making roles of couples. The study found that in many families, there is a division of financial duties. And this makes sense—we are all busy people, and there is a division of all duties in every household. Both partners don't take out the trash every week, right? We are busy people, so we divide and conquer. And when it comes to money, there are often two different roles for the household. You have the household CFO (Chief Financial Officer), whose primary responsibility is to make decisions on investments and create your financial plan. But in my experience, this person largely focuses on *Step 2: Creating a strategy to achieve your vision and become financially independent.* And the focus of the CFO is often to maximize returns and minimize taxes.[xiii]

These aren't bad aspirations; they just aren't complete. Think about this for a second. Do you want this on your tombstone?

Here Lies John Smith

He outperformed the market and reduced his tax burden.

My observation is that many people are so focused on their own strategy of how to make money, they don't see the potential of how their investments can facilitate the achievement of their vision—right now, today, not in "retirement."

The frequent partner to the household CFO is the COO "Chief Operating Officer"—the person who gets things done. The COO is making sure the bills are paid and managing the day-to-day expenses, and the million other tasks to manage in a household. We know from numerous studies that women are often the COO and take on a disproportionate burden of all household duties; they have an abundance of pressing responsibilities and a scarcity of time.

That is why it makes a lot of sense that *Step 1: Identifying your vision* gets overlooked. But identifying what you are investing for, aka your vision, is the most important thing you can do for your financial future. And Step 1 isn't a permanent commitment, it is something that changes as your life and circumstances change. And Step 1 requires zero financial literacy. Your vision has nothing to do with your investment strategy. In fact, your investment strategy is subservient to your vision. Defining your vision can be an activity that brings the CFO and COO together. Don't get me wrong, one of you may need to take the lead on starting to craft your vision, but once created, executing on that vision (i.e., saving more/making tradeoffs) can motivate both partners.

Saving more isn't just to save more money, investing isn't just to make more money; both are in service of achieving your vision. Without a vision, your daily choices around your finances are just that, daily choices without context. With a vision, every choice you make becomes a tradeoff. Is this choice getting me closer to our vision, or further away? Understand that the earlier in your life you spend a little time exploring your dreams, and your relationship with money, the greater chance you will have of achieving those dreams. Even if you aren't exactly sure of those dreams. Even if they will change, which they will.

Your vision will include both short and long-term goals

Your vision includes two elements: what you want your life to look like, and what you want the purpose of your life to be. Start with what you want your life to look like. Usually, it is easy to identify short-term goals, perhaps you want to eliminate credit card debt from your life. Or you have been planning a trip to Italy.

Long-term goals are more difficult to identify, which is completely understandable; how do any of us know what we want ten years from now, much less twenty or thirty years from now? But just because something is difficult, doesn't mean it isn't worth it. Identifying your long-term financial goals, i.e., what you want your money to do for you, in service of the life you want to lead, is an exercise that many people avoid. It isn't an easy exercise, but it can change your life. If you can start to identify your long-term goals, you can start to make financial choices to help you achieve those goals much more quickly than if you haven't identified your financial goals.

How do you determine your long-term financial goals?

We frequently see financial goals tied to possessions: I want to buy a house, a car, a designer bag, a boat, etc. These goals can be helpful, but are sometimes incomplete. When considering your financial goals, think about the life you want to lead, not just the stuff you want to have.

The financial industry loves to promote what they classify as the ultimate financial goal: "Retirement." Insert uplifting music and spotlights here. *Retirement* is consistently the number one rated long-term financial goal in many different investor studies. *Retirement* has become almost an obsession of the financial industry, with retirement income coming in at a close second. The amount of money, time and effort spent on discussing retirement, retirement products, how to get investors to save more for retirement is astronomical.

Underneath all of this is an assumption that retirement is a worthy financial goal, in and of itself. We assume that the concept of retirement is time-tested, prudent, and absolutely necessary for every individual. In the media, we see this headline over and over again (likely written and ready to run on a slow news day): "American's aren't saving enough for retirement." This repetitive headline is always followed by questionable statistics in a regurgitated article. Again, it's relatively easy to manipulate the data to tell the story you want to tell. And of course, the financial industry is happy to offer "solutions" to solve this looming "crisis." Many in the financial industry are paid on a percentage of the assets they manage, which is an imbedded incentive for them to push investors to keep saving and investing for retirement. But if we take a step back from the never-ending noise loop created by the financial industry, and promoted by financial media, retirement is a relatively new, untested experiment.

In America, the first time the government established an official program to provide a source of ongoing income to anyone was after the Civil War, to veterans, which made up less than 1% of the population when benefits started to be distributed in 1906. Social Security expanded the concept of providing guaranteed income to Americans based on their earnings, but Social Security is an even newer concept. Passed in 1935, Social Security provided guaranteed income to Americans once they reached a certain age. It's important to note that the intention of Social Security wasn't to begin an era of "retirement" for all senior citizens, as the average life expectancy for Americans in 1935 was 59.9. Based on when full benefits started (at age 65), the majority of Americans would die before receiving benefits.[xiv]

After World War II, we saw private companies increasingly provide employees with pension plans, another source of guaranteed income for retirees. By 1970, 45% of all private sector employees were covered by some type of pension plan.[xv] The concept of retirement really came to fruition after World War II, when rising life expectancies ensured a large number of Americans had access to two sources of guaranteed income after a thirty- or forty-year career.

The sources of guaranteed income:

1. A monthly check from the government (Social Security)

Supplemented by:

2. Pension plans (for both public and private workers), typically in the form of another monthly check.

But the dramatic increase in life expectancy of Americans has had a profound impact on this new experiment called retirement. In 1901, the average life expectancy was 49.1 years.[xvi] Fifty years later, in 1951, life expectancy shot up to 68.4, nearly a 40% increase. In 2022, it is up to seventy-seven years.[xvii] Retirement is a period of your life that could last up to thirty years (sometimes longer) that didn't even exist 100 years ago. That's nearly three decades of life on earth for the average American. The rise in life expectancy coincided with these two new sources of guaranteed income, ensuring that seniors would not have to be dependent on their adult children or work to survive. This is truly a remarkable change in the life stages of humans, all occurring in the past 100 years or so. And understandably, our understanding about what we do with nearly thirty extra years of our life is just beginning to form.

What does *Retirement* mean to you?

Retirement can mean a million different things to a million different people. Retirement could mean working part-time and living on a beach in a condo, or it could mean selling your house and possessions and traveling the world, or it could mean leaving work ten years earlier than you planned to care for your ailing parents.

Retirement is idealized by the financial industry as this "golden age" of your life, the reward for all your years of hard work. We've all seen the commercials accentuated by walks on the beach or a scene from a golf course or a sailboat. But if you look at the preliminary data, the initial results on this new, experimental thirty-year plan for your life are troubling. As the Magic 8 Ball would put it, "Outlook not so good."

Over the past twenty years, the divorce rate among older people has doubled. The divorce rate among people over sixty-five is rising even faster.[xviii] Among older adults, retirees are more likely to experience depression compared to those who are still working. People over age eighty-five have the highest rates of suicide.[xix] Am I suggesting that you don't retire? Not necessarily. What I am suggesting is that you do the hard work of creating a vision of the life you want to lead, and what you want your purpose to be, and you create your financial strategy based on that vision. This vision isn't something you wait until retirement to achieve; this vision is how you want to live your life. Right now.

It will take some time to define your vision, and there will likely be incremental steps you will need to take, but your vision can't wait. The unintended consequence of retirement is the temptation of later. Sacrifice now, we tell ourselves, to do what we want to do when we retire.

That book you want to write? You don't have to worry about it now, because that is what you will focus on in retirement.

That idea you have to help others? No need to start until you have your nest egg.

Unfulfilled in your job, relationships stressed? Sacrifice your life now, because you will have all the time you need in retirement.

Retirement unintentionally gives us permission to put off the difficult and important, to accept the mediocrity of now, under the guise of responsible self-sacrifice. All the while, there is no guarantee you will even make it there or have the physical and mental ability to do the things you want once you get there.

This is where the financial industry is steering folks in the wrong direction. Rather than fear-mongering, emphasizing longer-life expectancies and the need for more and more assets, the goal of a financial plan shouldn't be retirement, it should be focused on finding your vision for your life, identifying how you want to intentionally spend your time—not your time in retirement, your time now. You can absolutely save and prepare for retirement. You should use the tools of retirement accounts to reduce taxes, too, but retirement shouldn't be the primary focus of your financial plan, nor the number one priority.

Don't fall into the trap of focusing on retirement to the detriment of being intentional about how you are spending your time right now. How many times have you heard (or said), "where did the time go?"

I firmly believe the greatest financial plans are about your ENTIRE life, not just the last third of it. And that is the best place to start: creating a financial plan for your LIFE, not just your retirement. To determine your vision and become more intentional about how you spend your time.

And this gets me back to my original point: perhaps you are asking the wrong questions when it comes to your money. Because I can't answer your question about cryptocurrency, or I-bonds or any other technical question you have about finances until you've identified your unique vision, and how you uniquely want to spend your time.

You may be thinking: "Well, this all sounds great, but I have no idea how to figure out my vision. In fact, I've been pushed to make "responsible life choices" like getting a good job or saving for retirement by my parents, and by society my entire life!" Don't despair. In the next chapter, I am going to take you through some concrete and actionable exercises to help you clearly articulate what that vision looks like.

CHAPTER 6: CREATING YOUR VISION

Gratitude

At the end of class, the teacher will frequently suggest that you take a moment to give gratitude to everyone, including yourself, that helped you get on your mat today. What is one thing that you are grateful for? It could be a material possession, like your house, or a piece of clothing or furniture, a favorite picture. It could be a relationship, whether a family member (human or pet) or friend. It could even be something you experience, the flowers you see on a walk, the wind rustling through the trees, or the multitude of changing colors in the sky during magic hour.

Asking and answering the question, "What are you grateful for?" every day, and writing it down in a journal, can help you understand what is important to you. The expectations of the people around us, in our city or even our country, can establish boundaries for our lives that don't reflect what we value, but we stay within the boundaries because it is expected. It has taken me many years to separate "expected" vs. "wanted."

One of my inspirations for creating my vision was Catherine. Catherine is a yoga teacher I adore, who created a vision for her life in her twenties. Pretty amazing, but she created that vision only after graduating from law school and finding herself miserable working for a big law firm. She had spent so many years working, striving, sacrificing to become what was "expected" of her, but at what personal cost? She had the courage to take a step back, let go of her own expectations, expectations from her family and her colleagues and decide she wanted to live differently. She quit that prestigious job, became a yoga teacher, writer and several years later, a studio owner.

Expectations surround us, so much so that we don't even notice them. When you go out to eat, the restaurant sets the boundaries for your meal. Will it be a rich, heavy meal with a couple of large courses, or multiple courses with just a bite or two on each plate? Will it be a place where the food's appearance is just as important as how it tastes? The restaurant sets the boundaries, and the waiter is probably going to look at you funny if you ask for vegan options at a steakhouse. This may seem obvious, because you are choosing the restaurant, the experience. But cultures set boundaries that aren't necessarily questioned, especially if we haven't experienced a different way.

A recent example is corporate work before the pandemic. Most corporate cultures established the boundary that most, if not all, work should be done at the office. Few strayed from that boundary, and if you did, it was expected that you were limiting your career. But the pandemic illustrated that this boundary wasn't necessary. In fact, productivity soared working from home.

What are the boundaries or expectations you are following in your life that don't align with what you value? This question can be helpful when creating your vision.

Often discussions about money and investing focus on money and investing. These discussions can often miss the point. One of the first things you should determine is why you want to invest. A great place to start with this question is to picture what a life of financial independence would look like. This can be a difficult exercise, regardless of where you are in your life. But at the end of the day, you can't take your money with you; you can take your beautiful memories and life experiences that you created by clarifying your vision. Start to craft a picture of what you want your life to look like, and what you want your purpose to be, and together, these make up your financial vision.

First let's talk about what you want your life to look like. In order to be free to live the life you want, you have to achieve some level of financial independence. The five "W"s can help you create a better picture of what financial independence would look like for you. Here are just a few questions for you to get started. I'd encourage you to write down the answers to each of these questions. Don't overthink it, just write down what first comes to mind. If your writing causes additional thoughts or questions to come to mind, write down those answers too. This exercise shouldn't take more than ten to twenty minutes, and you will have time to reflect on the answers later.

WHO

Who do you want to spend your time with?

Who is it important for you to provide resources for/care for?

Are there any specific financial considerations concerning family members. This could include spouses, children, parents, etc.

Are there communities/groups beyond your family that you are drawn to/want to help?

WHAT

What would your ideal day, or month look like, unrestricted by money and obligation? Lying on a beach somewhere tropical may come to mind, and of course it's valid to picture vacation-like qualities in your ideal day. But remember, for many retirees, endless days of idle time aren't as enjoyable as they imagined.

Make a list of the activities that you love to do, including things you'd like to do, but just don't have the time for right now.

What do you like to do that helps other people?

What are you naturally good at doing?

What parts of your life are most meaningful to you?

What stresses you out that you would like to eliminate/change in your life?

WHEN

When do you want to achieve financial independence? When do you think you could achieve financial independence?

What are the barriers to achieving your vision for your life?

How can you overcome these barriers? Think creatively, consider things you've never considered before.

Are there any incremental steps you can take to get you closer to your vision?

What could a transition period look like? For example, if you have children or family members you are caring for, you may want to write down what your financially independent life may look like now, and how that could change when you have an empty nest.

WHERE

Many jobs and professions are no longer location dependent. Perhaps you ideally want to live in multiple locations. Think about the weather you love (and the weather you hate), if you gravitate toward urban or rural areas, location specific activities you enjoy, proximity to friends and family, and if you prefer to have a home base or to change locations frequently.

How important is it to you to live near your family? Outside your family, do you have friends or anyone else that it is important for you to live nearby?

Note any important requirements for any location (schools, availability of healthcare, etc.):

Where do you ideally want to live?

Before you make any change in locale, consider visiting a place you are considering for an extended period of time (four to six weeks) to get a better sense of the location. Is this an incremental step you want to include in your vision?

WHY

Why is your purpose in life. Your purpose in life is rooted in using what you have to help others.[xx] It's important to acknowledge that your purpose goes beyond your immediate circle of friends and family. Many scientific studies have found that a purpose rooted in helping others has numerous positive benefits, including less stress, better health, and even greater financial success.[xxi,xxii] You may find your purpose is to quit your full-time job now, but go back to work part-time five years from now, or your purpose may be to start a side hustle with the goal of it being your primary hustle, or maybe your purpose is to quit work at sixty-two and not just play golf, but volunteer to be a golf coach for your local high school team. Review the answers to the "Who," "What," "When," and "Where" questions and write a sentence or two summarizing what is most important/what sticks out to you from this exercise. If you feel uncertain about your answers or simply couldn't answer some of the questions, that is very normal. Focus on the answers you did complete, and what resonates the most with you. And note that this vision isn't set in stone, it will absolutely change as your circumstances change. Expect it to change over time. But if you don't even attempt to articulate a vision, you are guaranteed not to make progress toward the life you want to live. How could you make progress toward something you haven't yet established?

What sticks out/is most important from my WHO, WHAT, WHEN, WHERE answers?

My DRAFT Vision for my Life:

MY DRAFT Purpose for my Life:

Once you have a draft of your vision, recognize that your vision becomes your motivation for any financial changes you want to make. Achieving your complete vision typically takes time, but you can identify one quick win that you can achieve over the next twelve months.

What is one quick win that will get me closer to achieving my vision and my purpose in the next month? In the next twelve months?

Your vision is unique to you. Everyone has a different vision. Everyone's vision will have different time horizons and different funding costs. Step 2, your strategy to achieve your vision, will be specific to these unique differences. You wouldn't ask a builder what kind of materials you should use to build your house without letting them know the location, weather, and topography of the lot. But when you ask technical questions about investing before identifying your purpose, that is exactly what you are doing. And I'm not suggesting that you never ask the technical questions—you do want to understand the difference between a Roth and Traditional IRA—it is extremely helpful to understand the jargon-filled convoluted content that passes for financial communication. But don't start there. In my experience, many people who focus on technical questions never get to their vision.

    A vision can become your motivator for saving, or your motivator for investing. If you don't have a purpose, if you are just saving for *retirement* or because you are supposed to, depending on your attitudes and beliefs about money, you may be less motivated to save as much as you can. If you are already motivated to save, your vision can help you utilize (instead of hoarding) those assets to achieve your vision—you'll know what you're saving for. If you come up with a specific vision, let's say you'd like to own a retreat in Breckenridge and stay there for three months each year, and fly the entire family in every holiday, that can become a motivating factor to change your current behavior to accomplish your vision. If you don't have a vision, you can't make the changes necessary to make that vision a reality.

We always hear that "life happens" and "life will always happen"—there are always going to be things that impact our lives that are outside of our control. But the more we start to create what we want to happen, the more we write it down in specific terms, the more we start to see that it can become a reality.

Life happened for me in my job: How I fared without a vision

I was a corporate cog in the financial industry for over twenty-five years. How people relate to money, and how families relate to each other about money has fascinated me, and I wanted to teach people that spending time on their finances does not equate to enduring listening to someone drone on for sixty minutes about the financial markets. (And trust me, I have listened to my fair share of those presentations). Anything related to Step two, or learning how to invest, is just a means to an end. It is simply a way of achieving your vision more quickly. But at the end of the day, all of that is meaningless if it isn't tied to you and your vision. In my early thirties, I had a role that allowed me to conduct research and develop programs to help advisors, which I loved. But I hadn't taken the time or the effort to define my purpose. I honestly thought you were supposed to take any opportunity that was "climbing up the ladder."

And then...life happened; the financial crisis of 2008 hit. All financial firms were under tremendous financial stress, and many had to make significant layoffs. Jobs were scarce, so I was thankful to be at my firm. My firm adjusted our strategy, and my prior role was going away, but because I had been successful in my role, I was offered a different job with increasing responsibility. I was flattered by the offer and didn't really think about the implications. The new job focused on strategic marketing planning, a very different focus than my prior role.

It took me five tough years of increased dissatisfaction with my job for me to realize that I had taken an unintentional detour. Because I hadn't taken the time to define and write down my vision, I took what seemed to be a "great" opportunity and ended up miserable.

After waking up a few too many times simply dreading going to work, I took some time to really define what I wanted to do for the next few years, and also gave myself permission to think about what I really wanted to accomplish: what was my vision for my life? What I really loved was exploring the emotional aspects of money, understanding why people made the financial choices they did, and helping them make more intentional choices going forward.

When the financial crisis hit, I had a self-limiting belief that the only career for me was as an employee, that I needed to work for forty plus years and then I could start doing what I wanted when I "retired." I never would have dreamed of becoming the entrepreneur I am now. But starting to define what my career purpose was then, which focused on how I wanted to help others in my corporate job, started my journey to completely changing my life. It's OK that I didn't create the vision for my life that I'm living now. It was just the beginning of my journey.

Once I had defined my purpose and how I wanted to make a fairly dramatic career shift, it took me a while to share it with my boss. I was nervous, because it involved creating a new role that wasn't previously in the organization. But I had gradually changed from someone who was very engaged and fulfilled in my job to someone who dreaded coming into work every day, so I knew something needed to shift. I shared this idea for a new role with my boss, explaining my passion for exploring the emotional aspects of money, and making the case for how that work aligned with the goals of the firm.

As soon as I developed my purpose, I was suddenly able to advocate for a next step that brought me closer to my purpose, not just taking whatever opportunity to climb the ladder that came my way. Even though it took time to get where I wanted to go, I was no longer dreading going to work every day because I was on a path, and I was taking steps to get there. And it took even more "life happens" moments to get where I am today. But a specific purpose is inherently motivating. You'll be shocked by how clear things in your life become, how obvious what is no longer serving you, when you articulate that vision.

CHAPTER 7: YOUR FINANCIAL PERSONALITY

Non-attachment

Non-attachment simply means letting go of your expectations for how things should go. I travel frequently for work, and one of my favorite things to do is to take a yoga class in a studio in whatever city I happen to be in that day. Sometimes, the teacher will start class in a way I have never experienced before. I confess, sometimes I get annoyed. I think to myself, this is a ridiculous way to start class! I am especially triggered when we come into a pose that I have been in a thousand times before, but the teacher's instruction is the exact opposite, or even what was explicitly called out as incorrect, by prior teachers.

I immediately think to myself, they are doing it all wrong! And then, I have a choice to make. I can choose to be irritated, or I can choose to practice "non-attachment"—to let go of my preconceived notions of how things "should" go and be open to whatever I have been invited to experience. I may hate it, or I may discover something new. It's not easy. I am successful at letting go of my attachment sometimes, not all the time. But when I do, it can change my whole experience of class.

If you can become aware of your attachments around money and let go of your long-held beliefs that no longer serve you, you can have a completely different experience going forward. I invite you to let go of your "shoulds" and "supposed tos" and explore how things can be different if you are willing to let go.

Step 2, as we've discussed, is having a strategy to achieve your vision and become financially independent. This step gets too much time and attention already. We are going to skip this for now and come back to it after we cover step 3.

Before you execute your strategy, you need to understand your personal attitudes toward your finances, and identify your strengths and struggles. This reminds me of the prep that goes into painting a room. You can spend more time prepping a room, by taping the trim and windows, than you spend actually painting. Sure, you can skip the tape, but you are going to end up with a much better end result if you spend a little time up front to prep. Spending the prep time to better understand your financial personality will help you make better financial choices.

Financial choices are not made in a vacuum. Understanding the financial personalities of the people you love can benefit both your finances and your relationships. If you have a partner, have them go through the following exercise too and look at your combined strengths and struggles.

Why is understanding your financial personality important?

I've presented about financial personalities hundreds of times to thousands of diverse people. Invariably, someone will come up to me after my talk, just bursting to tell me how much my session resonated with them. The topic of finance is mired with so much judgement upon investor decisions, and an abundance of charts and graphs that are difficult to understand; much of the content has no connection to the everyday experiences people have with money. And the choices you make each and every day can have a tremendous impact on ultimate wealth. At the same time, the financial industry struggles with helping people make good choices. There is the whole academic discipline called "behavioral economics"; the discipline's main tenant is that people don't behave rationally around money.[xxiii,xxiv]

The myopic focus on charts, graphs and numbers, and the absence of meaningful insight on WHY people make irrational decisions about money is a big issue with the financial industry. It's an industry that focuses on numbers and forgets about people. There is such an emphasis on quantitative analysis to attempt to explain what just happened to the market, or where the market is headed, that they forget that we are human beings. The fact that an academic discipline was created to explain that humans don't act rationally just illustrates how out of touch the industry is with humanity!

It is no great surprise that people don't make rational decisions on a number of choices in their lives, way beyond finance. But financial advisors make recommendations to their clients and can't understand why their clients don't take their advice. That is the gap I'm trying to address: helping people understand their inherent beliefs about money so they can be more intentional about their choices moving forward. Because the consequences of irrational financial behavior can be devasting.

Estate planning can be a huge source of pain (above and beyond losing a loved one) for families. There are many, many people, for a myriad of reasons, who don't plan for the effective distribution of their assets after they die. The results are often extremely unfortunate. Assets can get tied up in long and costly probate processes. Worst of all, families are torn apart because each family member thinks they know what the person who died wanted to have happen with their estate.

The last episode of the HBO series *Succession* plays this out to a tee. Each child honestly believes their father wanted them to run the company. We can only guess how much Kendall, Shiv and Roman's relationship suffers after their father's death. The show illustrates that death is the most taboo and difficult financial topic of them all. Despite the fact that Logan Roy is a billionaire, has a depth of resources, lawyers, and advisors, he never effectively planned his estate or communicated his wishes. Chaos ensued.

I've observed that once people go through an extremely negative financial experience, directly tied to irrational decisions, they become open to changing their behaviors going forward. In one research effort, there was a gentleman, let's call him Dan, who was the executor of his uncle's estate. Even though his uncle had accumulated a significant amount of wealth, his estate was a complete mess. Dan described his uncle as "somewhat paranoid"; he would never talk to anyone in his family about his money. Once Dan started working on the estate, he quickly realized it was a nightmare. There were accounts all over the place, money stashed in weird places in the house. It took Dan two years to sort out the estate. Dan lamented the worst part— because his uncle had never created a record of his assets, there could still be assets out there that Dan simply didn't locate.

But what happened next was the silver lining. Dan, who had previously never spoken to his two adult daughters about his finances, decided to challenge his previously held attitudes and jump into very uncomfortable territory. Before this experience, Dan would never dream of having a conversation with his daughters about his finances, it was simply none of their business! But after the experience with his uncle, he sat down with his two daughters and reviewed his finances and estate plan, because he didn't want them to go through what he did when he handled his uncle's estate.

Remember when I shared the story about people "breaking the fourth wall" in my research efforts, convinced they would change their behavior as a result of simply attending a focus group? One of those groups heard Dan's story firsthand. I believe hearing the potential negative outcomes (in real scenarios, not fictional TV shows) can be a powerful motivator. Many people aren't aware of the issues that can occur without both planning and communicating your wishes for your estate. Many people haven't even had the experience of dealing with any estate, so hearing a story like Dan's can be eye opening.

IDENTIFYING YOUR FINANCIAL PERSONALITY

Over the many years that I've researched investors, I've learned a few things. First, we all have unique attitudes and beliefs about money, often influenced by early childhood experiences. But families don't all have the same financial personalities. Many times, our loved ones, even if they were raised in the same environment as we were (a great example is siblings) can have very different attitudes and beliefs about money.

Everyone that interacts with money is a human, and often we make decisions based on both logic and emotion. However, our attitudes and beliefs about money are often unexamined. We don't necessarily know *why* we react the way we do when it comes to financial events (good and bad) in our lives. That is why I have created the financial personality model, to help individuals better understand their relationship with money. Your unconscious beliefs can predict your income and net worth. You have the ability to change your financial behaviors, but first you must understand your unconscious beliefs about money. Once you understand how you might initially react, you can recognize your habitual reflex, pause, and change that reaction.

The first step in understanding your relationship with money is to reflect on your own personal experiences with money. Write down the answer to these questions. Don't think about it too much, just write down what first comes to you.

1. What are some of your earliest memories about money? Write down up to three of your earliest money memories.

2. Do you remember any stories your family told that involved money?

3. Write down some of the lessons or sayings you learned about money when you were growing up. Did you accept or reject these money lessons?

Ideally take a day or two to reflect on how those memories have impacted your relationship with money before moving on to the next section.

The Financial Personality Model

Once you have explored your childhood experiences with money, let's connect those experiences to your attitudes around money today. The first dynamic to explore is your mindset when it comes to your personal finances. We will explore here both SCARCITY and ABUNDANCE mindsets.

An easy way to think about these two different mindsets is from a generational perspective. Our unique attitudes and beliefs about money are shaped by our personal experiences. Generations collectively experience world events, although your personal experience might be very different than someone else in your generation. We are all members of a generation, and are all privy to the collections of ideals and stereotypes, the profile, our generation has been given. Some of those attributes resonate with us deeply, others, less so. Just because you are a member of a generation doesn't mean you are the same as the majority in your generation, but generational generalities (say that three times fast) can be helpful.

My Great Aunt Nadine personified the scarcity mindset. Her generation was very skeptical of the stock market and financial institutions in general, and many were extreme savers. When I reflect on her life, her attitudes about money were greatly impacted by her childhood experiences, because Aunt Nadine grew up in the Great Depression. If we think we are living in economically uncertain times now, the Great Depression was on a different scale entirely. We may be concerned about stock markets, or inflation, but many Americans who went through the Great Depression were concerned on a daily basis with having enough to eat. Many government safety net programs were created as a response to the lack of safety nets for many Americans during that time.

The Great Depression was the worst economic disaster in American history. Many Americans lost their entire life savings when their local bank failed (there was no government program that guaranteed your deposits). Nearly 25% of the workforce was unemployed, and there were no unemployment benefits that they could collect. The Great Depression lasted for years. Just to get a sense of how much this economic event disrupted Americans, farmers dealing with the great dust bowl would leave their farms and migrate to a different part of the country to look for work.[xxv]

The Great Depression impacted my Aunt Nadine for her entire life. She never fully trusted banks, she was extremely reluctant to spend money on anything, and she had a healthy fear that something bad was about to happen (like another Great Depression). She was extremely frugal, careful when spending money to get the best "deal" and always knew exactly how much money she did have. I'm not saying that Aunt Nadine was a pessimist, but she always wanted to be prepared for the worst-case scenario. She never felt totally comfortable, no matter her current financial situation.

This may be surprising, but many Gen Xers and Millennials have a scarcity mindset. They have had many negative, destabilizing experiences when it comes to money and investing, including the dot.com bust, 9/11, and the global financial crisis. They have had a very different experience than Baby Boomers when it comes to personal finances. Tack on two decades of war, a global pandemic and the looming impact of climate change and you have a group that feels very uncertain about the future.

Millennials have never experienced a bull market, a period of extended market outperformance. They came of age in increasingly volatile and uncertain investment times, and their attitude about investing is very different than their Baby Boomer parents. Millennials are focused on spending less and saving more, two attributes of a scarcity mindset.

They relate to Aunt Nadine's feelings of "keep what you have"—you never know when the other shoe is going to drop. I can't tell you how many Millennials have come up to me, in almost a cathartic way, after I describe the scarcity mindset, to share that I have described them exactly.

Investing, to Millennials, is almost a leap of faith, as they haven't personally experienced the gains prior generations have enjoyed. Yet, Millennials get chastised for being too "risk averse." Rather than assuming they have a long-time horizon to accumulate wealth, they are often scared about what unknown calamities the future holds.

The good news is that most individuals who have a scarcity mindset are great savers. Aunt Nadine never threw away anything. When you have a scarcity mindset, your brain rewards you when you accumulate something. When you see your account balance go up, your brain gets a dopamine hit. When you are trying to accumulate wealth, having a scarcity mindset provides you with a great advantage, because the more you save, the more you have. Pretty obvious, right? The less obvious downside is that savers can sometimes have a tough time spending what they've accumulated.

Some savers don't know how to stop saving, and the prospect of spending has the opposite effect of the good feeling they have when saving, and this isn't exclusively tied to money. When you have a scarcity mindset, it is important to write down specific dollar amounts for financial goals. Often when you have a scarcity mindset and achieve a financial goal, you simply move the goal post. You have the potential to never have "enough," no matter how much you have saved. There is a balance between saving to secure your future, and enjoying the fruits of your hard-earned savings with the people you love.

In summary, individuals with a scarcity mindset are typically savers. They will do everything in their power not to waste resources. This saving behavior can extend to things as well as money. For some with a scarcity mindset, it can be difficult to throw things with potential utility away, as they don't want to get rid of anything they can potentially use down the road. On the other side of the road are individuals with an abundance mindset.

How abundance and scarcity mindsets think differently

I spend a lot of time on the road, and road warriors can spend way too much time discussing and even bragging about their status levels with various travel reward programs. This can seem ridiculous, but reward programs are the crumbs frequent travelers hold onto when they are spending yet another night away from home. My friend Andy and I were at an airport, waiting out yet another flight delay, when we started talking about which hotels and airlines had the best reward programs. Andy proudly shared with me the account balances he had accumulated at his two favorite loyalty programs: over a million points each. I could tell just by the way he wanted me to see his balances, he actually pulled up the apps and pointed them out to me, that these balances gave him great pleasure.

As someone with an abundance mindset, I immediately started to dream about what fabulous trips he could take with these balances! But when I suggested an amazing hotel to spend some of those points on, it was clear that Andy wasn't planning on using any of those points anytime soon, if ever.

This blows my mind, because even though I have done a great job changing my spending habits, I tend to view points as "free"—and although I've accumulated millions of points, I would never have a million points at any reward program, because I use them all the time to my great pleasure.

In my conversation with Andy, I realized his joy was in accumulating the points—being able to look at his million-dollar account balances. Spending the points wouldn't be that enjoyable to him because he would also know his points balance would go down. Many, not all individuals with an abundance mindset are spenders rather than savers. Spenders' brains reward them when they spend money. If you have an abundance mindset, you expect your wealth and success to continue to grow.

Baby Boomers, in general, have an abundance mindset. Of course, there are always exceptions; not all Baby Boomers have an abundance mindset.

Individuals with an abundance mindset tend to think the best is yet to be. Bill Clinton's campaign song was Fleetwood Mac's "Don't Stop" with an upbeat chorus that chimed, "Don't stop thinking about tomorrow…"

It's almost laughable to think about that song inspiring Millennials to vote for a candidate. You can imagine Millennials "thinking about tomorrow" as a dystopian landscape of "The Walking Dead" rather than a bright future with sunshine and rainbows.

It is too simplistic to say that people with an abundance mindset are optimists. If we look more closely at Baby Boomers, their experiences support their belief that things just get better. They experienced increasing personal wealth in both real estate and the stock market. Forward progress seems inevitable, not accidental to those with an abundance mindset. I'm not suggesting that hardships aren't experienced, but those with an abundance mindset see hardships as something that they will most certainly overcome.

Let's look more closely at Baby Boomers' experiences with real estate. In the early 60s, it was much more affordable to purchase a house than it is today. Many Baby Boomers were in their twenties in the 1960s. If we look at the year 1965, the median price of a home in the United States was a little over $20,000. Over the years, the value of Baby Boomers' homes increased dramatically. In fact, the median price of a home at the end of

2020, fifty-five years later was $324,900. Baby Boomers personal experience with real estate made them believe buying a home was a source of abundance as well as a good investment.[xxvi]

But if we look at Millennials, their experience with buying a home has been completely different. When I'm speaking about investing to groups, I'll ask the Millennials in the audience what their first big impression of investing in real estate was, and the universal answer is…2008. Many Millennials don't think buying a home is a good investment; they see it as an increasingly unaffordable burden that may or may not ever pay off for them. And that same scarcity mindset extends to the stock market.

Let me pause right here and mention that neither mindset is right or wrong, better or worse than the other. It's simply the result of your personal experiences.

The first dynamic of your financial personality is your money *mindset.*

Do you have an ABUNDANCE or SCARCITY mindset?

MINDSET

SCARCITY ⟵—————⟶ ABUNDANCE

When thinking about your money mindset, it's helpful to view this dynamic on a scale of one to ten. One is an extreme scarcity mindset, and ten is someone with an extreme abundance mindset. Some people might rate themselves a two, others might be a nine, but a lot of people fall somewhere in the middle. Decide where your tendency falls in most situations. And if you are having difficulty deciding between one dynamic versus another, perhaps you are right in the middle, say a five, on that ten-point scale. The good news is that folks in the middle have the greatest ability to change their reactions or decisions going forward on that specific dynamic.

The second dynamic is your *approach* to your finances.

Do you EMBRACE investing and spending time on your finances? Or do you AVOID thinking about your finances?

APPROACH

EMBRACE   AVOID

⟵—————————————⟶

How do you approach your finances in general, and how do you approach financial goals? Do you embrace and enjoy working on your finances? Do you make time to review potential new investment opportunities? Or is the topic of money and investing one that you avoid or are reluctant to discuss?

An individual that identifies at ten on this scale might not want to think or talk about their finances at all. Another individual that rates themselves as a one might spend time on their investments daily and feel very open to discussing investing. One point of clarification: your comfort level discussing money in situations with close family members (partner/children) can vary from your natural dynamic. Your unique, specific family dynamics have the most influence on your willingness to discuss (or not) your personal finances with your family. That is a topic for an entirely different book.

Putting these two dynamics together creates four different financial personalities. One is no better or worse than the other, but understanding which financial personality you most identify with can help you better understand your past money decisions and gives you the opportunity to make more intentional choices going forward.

FINANCIAL PERSONALITY MODEL

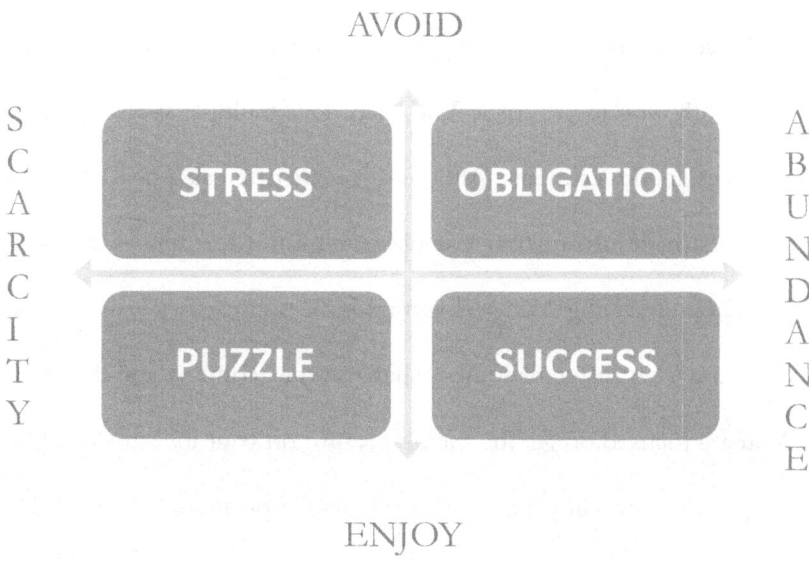

Brief overview of the four different financial personalities

We'll first describe the four financial personalities; then, once you've identified which personality you identify most closely with, we'll break down some beneficial tips for your money personality. First let's start with those who have a scarcity mindset. If you embrace your finances, money and investing is like a puzzle you can solve. But if you avoid finances, money is a great source of stress to you. Let's look a little more closely at these two financial personalities.

To You, Money is… **A Puzzle**

This money personality identifies those with a scarcity mindset who embrace their finances. Your personal finances are a puzzle that you are constantly working to solve. You likely have multiple spreadsheets on your finances and investments. Although you are often skeptical of new sources of investment information, you ultimately enjoy learning as much as you can about investing. You seek out multiple points of view and often compare what different sources share on the economy and the markets. You are focused on getting the best return on your investments, but keeping investment expenses down is also important.

It is very important to you to have "enough" money to guard against future needs and safeguard your family. You have several different financial goals for yourself and your family. Once you have achieved a financial goal, you find yourself either increasing the goal or setting a new financial goal. In terms of what/how you buy things, you are very aware of how much things cost. You know where to get the best prices for certain things. Saying "no" to spending is not difficult for you. It can be difficult for you to understand why people make choices you perceive as "wasting money."

To You, Money is… **Stress**

This money personality identifies those who have a scarcity mindset and avoids thought or conversation about money as much as possible. Money has always been a source of stress in your life. You are concerned that you "won't have enough"—and you can be hypervigilant about your finances. Regardless of the state of your current finances, you are waiting for the other shoe to drop.

Thinking about your financial plan is the last thing you want to do. You are concerned you will make the wrong investment choices. You are worried that a wrong choice could have a huge negative impact on your finances, so you often delay making those decisions.

The markets stress you out and you have this constant feeling in the back of your head that you could lose it all. Investing can seem more like gambling than wealth creation. Money can sometimes leave a bad taste in your mouth, as you think that money has the potential to corrupt. It can take you a long time to make a decision to purchase something. You won't buy something if you can get it cheaper somewhere else, even if it is less convenient. You believe it is wrong to spend a lot of money on things. Sometimes you feel guilty when you realize someone is a very hard worker but has a lot less than you or your family.

Now, let's review the two financial personalities with an abundance mindset. If you embrace your finances, you believe money represents success. If you avoid money and investing, your finances feel like an obligation.

To You, Money is… **Success**

This money personality identifies those with an abundance mindset who embrace their finances. Money is a reflection of your success. You are excited about opportunities to grow your wealth, including new businesses or investment opportunities. Getting the "best return" on your investments is important to you. Sometimes you may have a chip on your shoulder—your wealth is a "fuck you" to those who doubted you.

You enjoy reaping the benefits of your hard work, including having "the best" of things that are important to you. You are generous and help other family members when financial issues come up. You are not that concerned about how much things cost, and you don't like to be perceived as cheap/stingy. Gambling can be exciting to you. You relate to this statement: "I work hard, so I can play hard."

To you Money is… an **Obligation**

This money personality identifies those who have an abundance mindset but avoid their finances. You don't like to think about your finances, and you really don't like talking about money. Conversations about money don't interest you. You feel uncomfortable and sometimes intimidated when discussing investing. You enjoy spending money, either buying things you want or spending money on experiences like travel. When you are shopping, you quickly decide what you are going to buy.

You may think that if you worry too much about making money, you are not a great person. If you work hard enough, you believe things will work out financially. Sometimes you are resentful of extremely wealthy people. After all, money corrupts.

THINGS TO KEEP IN MIND

Once you have identified which financial personality you are, each personality has different things that can be beneficial to keep in mind regarding their finances and the choices you make every day regarding money.

Puzzle Personality Tips

Find a balance between your budget and your own enjoyment. Are you denying yourself or your family things you need or desire because you don't want to spend money? It's a common experience for some individuals in this personality to have saved more than enough to be financially independent and still live well below their means. They put off having that family trip, or even having that elective surgery that could have a positive impact on their life, even though they can easily afford it, because they don't want to spend the money. They have been rewarded for their frugality their entire lives and can't seem to fully enjoy the fruits of their labor. If any of this resonates with you, consider a spending goal. If you just made a face reading that, (a goal to spend????) keep reading! Think about a trip, experience, or purchase that you and your family have been considering for a while. Write a list of reasons why you should make the purchase, and then write a list of reasons why you shouldn't. If the purchase is a net positive, write down what is holding you back, or what conditions would need to be present for you to make the purchase.

Understand that you are likely the most extreme saver in your family. Budgets can be helpful with family members to ensure everyone is on the same page. Don't admonish family members for making purchases if they are staying within budget. Understand that other family members may feel judged by you.

In terms of your financial plan and financial goals, notice if you are moving the goal posts financially, and can't seem to save/have "enough." Your knowledge and enthusiasm are tremendous gifts to share with younger family members and the next generation. Find ways to share your love of investing with the next generation. (There are some ideas you can use later in this book).

Stress Personality Tips

A key thing you can do to lower your stress about money is to create a security blanket. Ask yourself: what would it take for you to feel safe and secure financially? That could be having six to twelve months of expenses in cash in an emergency fund, or it could be eliminating any debt. Your security blanket could be owning your own home, having a secure job, or some combination of options.

Identify what should be in your security blanket, and if this appeals to you, create a visual reminder of the security blanket, so you know it is there for you if you need it. Perhaps it could be a green throw blanket, or a picture of your house, or whatever physical representation that you can look at when feeling stressed about your finances.

Your security blanket helps you give yourself both ease and permission to invest for longer-term goals, and more importantly, flexibility when things don't go as planned. For example, if you are concerned about making an investment in real estate or the market, if you have your security blanket, you will have access to money if you unexpectedly need it. You won't have to touch your investment, and can leave it in for the long-term, giving it the best chance to grow over time.

Beware of unintentional limitations you put on yourself because of your need for security. In my life, part of my security blanket was having health insurance. A corporate job was a default (un-intentional) decision for many years, as I didn't believe I could afford health insurance otherwise.

Notice if you are putting off financial decisions, specifically because you don't want to make a "mistake." Not deciding or taking action can be a mistake in and of itself. Give yourself permission to not "have" to be an expert, or consider working with an advisor that can help guide you. Another option is to take advantage of products that do the work for you, such as target-date or asset allocation products. If you have a specific financial action you need to take but haven't, set a daily reminder in your calendar to sound an annoying noise until you complete the action. Once you complete the action, give yourself a little reward.

Not watching your investments every day is OK; in fact it is something I recommend, especially if you are investing for long-term goals. Watching and stressing about daily ups and downs of the market is a fruitless, often counter-productive exercise if you are a long-term investor, because daily movements have little to do with long-term results. I review my investments a few times a year, not every day.

Success Personality Tips

When exploring new investment options, slow down. Make decisions more slowly than you want. The more certain you think something is a "sure thing," or that you have knowledge that others don't, the slower you should proceed, and the harder you should question yourself. Getting the opinion of an independent third party, like a financial advisor, can provide potential downsides you haven't identified. FOMO often produces subpar returns. It's OK if your investment portfolio is boring—the new "hot opportunity" isn't always hot or a real opportunity. Conversely, don't overvalue/hold on to an investment solely because you think you "should" get more than the market is valuing it at right now.

Take the time to create your visions and include "moonshot" goals; this can give you added motivation to save and cultivate your ambition for your vision. Find a physical reminder of your vision that you can see every day. You have the drive and passion to achieve incredible goals, but you can also spend money aimlessly if you don't have a specific goal to save toward. Unsubscribe from notifications, texts and emails from marketers for products that don't align with your vision.

You are a generous person. You may need to set boundaries with friends or family. Sometimes you give money to others, even if you can't afford it.

Obligation Personality Tips

Explore why money is such an uncomfortable topic for you. Go back to your earliest money memory—was it a negative experience? Do you see any patterns in your finances that relate to this money memory? Once I made the connection in my own life that "we can't afford it" became "you are not worth it" to me personally; noticing this connection freed me to have a different connection with spending money. Saving my money, so I could achieve the life I wanted became my new expression of my self-worth. And I didn't feel deprived or upset when I spent less. Think of money like exercise, sometimes you hate it, but it is a tool to help you get where you want to be.

Sometimes you buy things on impulse, and perhaps regret or don't even use the purchase. The twenty-four-hour rule is a great practice to curb impulse spending. When you have the impulse to make a purchase over a pre-determined dollar amount, don't decide yes or no on the item, just wait twenty-four hours before deciding. You will frequently forget all about an impulse buy, but if you are still thinking about the item twenty-four hours later, it is something to consider purchasing.

The good news is that you don't need to spend a lot of time on money or become an expert to manage your finances effectively. If you are starting from square one, consider getting the help of a financial advisor. Knowing that you don't like to spend time on your finances, automating financial decisions or setting up notifications for tasks you can't automate is an easy way to make progress toward your financial goals with very little effort. When you reach a financial goal, take time to celebrate.

Now that you know your financial personality, how can you change your relationship with money going forward?

The thoughts in our brain are often habitual. Habits help us be efficient when completing tasks but can also be all-consuming. Have you ever felt like you couldn't "turn off" the to-do list in your brain? Or spent time recalling an upsetting conversation with a friend over and over and over again? Our brain is like any other muscle; without intentional exercise, it isn't as strong as it could be. And ironically, giving our thoughts "a break" is a way to exercise our brain. Thoughts come and go. Focusing on certain thoughts gives them more prominence. But you have the choice to let thoughts go that don't serve you. But just like anything else, you have to practice.

Changing your relationship with money begins with recognizing your habitual thoughts when it comes to money and investing. These are phrases or sentences you say to yourself repeatedly about money. Some examples could be:

"Don't ask anyone for anything, you can't trust anyone."

"That's too expensive."

"I only want my money in something safe."

"I deserve it" or "I don't deserve it."

"If only we had more money, things would be easier."

Write down your habitual thoughts about money:

Start to notice when your habitual thoughts about money come up routinely in your life. For example, maybe your partner spends money on things you wouldn't. Acknowledge that a thought habit such as thinking, "Why did you waste money on that?" isn't helping anything, assuming your partner is staying within a budget you both agreed upon.

Try to notice when a habitual thought comes into your head, and practice letting the thought go. We let go of thoughts all the time; think of the last time you were deep in thought, then a moment later questioning, *what was I just thinking?*

There are many ways to let thoughts go. In yoga, when we are experiencing discomfort (perhaps holding a pose for a really loooonnnnggg time), we notice the thoughts that come in our mind (*I hate this teacher!!!* or *I can't hold this pose any longer!*) and then get curious as to what is happening in our body. Are you clenching your jaw? Did your stomach muscles get tense? Are your shoulders up by your ears?

When you get curious about your body's reaction to stress, it gives you a little space from your thoughts. And then perhaps you take a deep breath, and you let that thought go.

How does this translate to your money? Let's take the experience of investing in the stock market for a long-term goal. There will be periods of time when you look at your account, and the value has gone down. This can be stressful. You may be tempted just to cut your losses and move into cash. For a long-term goal, staying the course through the short-term ups and downs on the market is a wise strategy for growing your wealth. Trying to time the market or abandoning your strategy because of a short-term dip is a recipe for failure. The next time you are stressed out because of the market, notice your thoughts.

Try not to go down a thought train (*Oh no, my account is down so much. I'm never going to be able to make this up. I can't deal with the market anymore. I'm never going to be able to retire…*).

Right after that first thought or reaction to your balance, let it go and start to notice how your body is reacting to this stressful situation. Approach the exercise with curiosity. Ask yourself—how is my body reacting to this stress? You can take a minute to scan your body methodically, from head to toe, to see what each part of your body is doing or feeling at that moment. Perhaps your initial thought is gone. But if it is still circling your brain, take a deep breath (or three or four) and see if you can let those thoughts go. Your thoughts aren't going to change the situation. But you do have the ability to change your reaction to the situation.

This doesn't work like an on/off switch. You likely won't have immediate relief or results, but over time, you can start to notice your thoughts, and give yourself a little space before your thoughts start to spiral.

There are lots of ways you can create some space between yourself and your thoughts the next time you experience a great amount of discomfort around a financial situation. Here are a couple ideas to create space:

1. Take your favorite exercise class
2. Listen to music
3. Meditate
4. Engage in your favorite hobby
5. Talk a long walk

Start with something you enjoy doing, otherwise, you aren't going to do it. And by the way, watching TV or looking at your phone doesn't count. It needs to be an activity that takes you away from your daily schedule. And often, breathing is more apparent when you are doing this activity. That can be helpful, as your breath is the simplest tool for letting habitual thoughts go. Simply imagine the thought dissolving as you exhale. And the thought may come right back on your next inhale, and that is perfectly normal. You are just beginning the practice of giving yourself space. This is something that just takes practice, like learning how to juggle. You are probably not going to get it right away, but you will start to notice small improvements over time.

CHAPTER 8: BECOMING FINANCIALLY INDEPENDENT

Balance

Let's try something. If you are able, put this book down right now, set your timer on your phone for one minute, and balance on one foot.

How was it? If it isn't so easy for you, let's try a couple things. If you have on shoes or socks, take them off. Stand back up and lift all ten toes, and then shift left and right, back and forth, until you find four spots on the bottom of your feet that help stabilize you. There are two spots towards the front of your foot, one on the left and the other on the right of the pad just below your toes, and two on each side of your heel. In yoga, they call these the four corners of your feet. These four corners literally help ground you.

Another great stabilizer that helps with balance is our core. To engage your core muscles, zip them up the same way you would zip up a pair of tight jeans. You have found the four corners of your feet. You've engaged your core. Let's try to balance on one foot again. This time, purposely try to find your edges, just until you feel you might fall down. Maybe you wave your arms around, maybe you close your eyes, there are a lot of ways to challenge your balance. It can be a humbling experience, or if you are having a good day with your balance, you may feel accomplished. Wow—I just did that?

If you are in a class of yogis, there is typically someone having a balance-challenged day (usually me) and someone who moves in and out with graceful ease. It is fun to watch someone with great balance.

What on earth does standing on one foot have to do with money? Make sure your financial plan has two feet on the ground. Maybe more. While balancing can be fun, no one wants to feel unsteady for an extended period of time. A very simple truth: it is easier to stand on two feet than one. And when we can control our own body, using our core, it can be easy to stand on one foot. But what we can't control is our environment. Uneven bricks and windy conditions can make balance more difficult.

If we are on a bouncy airport shuttle, we may even need three points of contact (grabbing on to a strap or handrail) to make sure we feel steady. So, having multiple stabilizers, i.e., points of contact, will make your financial situation feel much steadier. Even when the environment feels like a bouncy shuttle.

A good financial plan has at least two, perhaps three stabilizers. These stabilizers help you not to "fall down" financially. And when you have stabilizers, you feel steady even when things happen unexpectedly that you can't predict. Which is always going to happen.

Now that you have learned your financial personality and have a better awareness of why you have made past financial choices, you can start to become more intentional with your future financial choices. This is the right frame of mind to dive into Step 2: Creating your strategy to achieve your vision and become financially independent.

As I've shared before, most financial content focuses almost exclusively on step two. This chapter is a far cry from a complete overview of investing and financial planning. There are plenty of other resources you can access for this information. What follows is what I think is most important for you to know right now.

Focus first on the four factors that you control, and that have the greatest impact on achieving financial independence:

1. How much you can save and invest. (i.e., budget surplus, or **BS**).
2. How many **stabilizers** you need to feel financially secure.
3. How much **time** you have to invest.
4. Create your **investment strategy**

If you feel overwhelmed or naturally tend to avoid finances, you should also ask yourself: Does it make sense to get **help**? You can absolutely DIY these four steps, and you absolutely don't have to DIY the four steps. There are many resources that can help, and I will share exactly how you can get the help you need. Even if you decide to get help, I recommend reading the following overview, so you are familiar with the concepts and can communicate effectively with whomever assists you.

1. **Why is your budget (BS) so important? And what can I do to maximize BS?**

Your monthly budget surplus is essentially how much money you have after you've paid your fixed expenses (housing/transportation/food/debt).

If you aren't sure what your BS is, it's never been easier to find out. There are several budget apps, and most banks and credit cards offer easy ways to track your spending automatically. Less is more in terms of categories, ideally five to seven in total. If you've never looked at your budget before, it can be eye opening to see how much money you spend on certain categories each month.

If you are overwhelmed, in debt, or don't know where to start, a financial advisor or a credit counselor can help you create a budget; they will often review your spending and suggest ways to increase your BS. This could include ideas to increase your income as well as ways to reduce expenses.

Your financial vison also helps you maximize your BS. The more concrete vision you have of the life you want to lead, after achieving financial independence, the easier it is to make changes to your daily financial choices. Once you know your budget surplus, decide how much you want to invest and create an automatic transfer from your bank account to your investments, on the same day you get paid every month.

2. **How many stabilizers do you need to feel financially secure?**

We started this exercise earlier on in the book when I asked you to think about what it takes for you to feel safe and secure financially. But recognizing that women perceive risk and investing differently than men, I think it is important to ensure you are fulfilling your security needs. Fulfilling your security needs helps you make decisions beneficial to your long-term financial plan, even when it feels like the sky is falling in all around you.

An emergency fund is the first stabilizer everyone should have. It is a stabilizer for so many different reasons. It gives peace of mind that you have the resources to deal with an unexpected event. It gives you flexibility in a time when your finances may be under pressure. If you have an emergency fund, you won't be "forced" to take a job you don't want, or sell an asset at exactly the wrong time, or put an unexpected expense on a credit card because you can use your emergency fund.

How much should you put into your emergency fund? If you don't have one already established, start with $1000. Once you have that, begin to save six to twelve months of expenses. But if that isn't enough to meet your security needs, determine the amount that works for you. For those of you with a scarcity mindset, be mindful of how much is enough, and the tradeoffs you make for "safety."

How can you feel safe financially?

I mentioned the fact that no one asks your risk tolerance when you buy your house (arguably one of the biggest investments most people make in their lives). It can be useful to think about your strategy to achieve your vision in the same way an architect thinks about constructing a building. Obviously, the larger the building, the more complicated the plans. And safety is a critical part of any building plan. Just like there are no guarantees of safety in your house, or any building, that doesn't mean you can't take steps to ensure you have made things as secure as possible.

The safety strategies used in buildings are a good analogy for strategies you can employ in your financial plan. If you have a building with multiple stories, you will have elevators as well as stairs. Elevators are typically going to get you to your destination more quickly than stairs. Elevators are more expensive to purchase, and require much more ongoing maintenance than stairways, but they also save a tremendous amount of time and effort, especially if you look at the lifetime of a building, a very long period. Elevators are less reliable, particularly in an emergency, than stairways. That is not to say that people can't fall down a stairway, but if you look at the emergency evacuation plans for a building, they are going to suggest you take the stairs.

You can think of your investments as the elevators in your financial plan. Holding cash or money market funds are your staircases (or stabilizers). Investments are a little more expensive, require ongoing maintenance, but over the long term, the benefits outweigh the costs. Stairs are more reliable but are going to take you much longer to get where you want to go. The taller the building, the more effort it is to take the stairs. But architects don't choose one or the other, they put both in their buildings.

The question of whether or not to invest is not something to agonize over. Yes, of course you should invest. But you should have elevators and stairs in your investment portfolio. The elevator represents your investments, which have the potential for higher returns over the long term, but the value of your investments could go up and down in the short term. You are OK with having elevators, because you know you have the stability of stairs as well.

What does the staircase represent? What I call "stable" investments. These are investments that likely won't produce very high returns (less than 2%) but you have the security of knowing your account value will remain stable and easily accessible if you need it. This could be cash or high-yield savings accounts. Another type of a relatively "stable" investment is the bond market. When investing in the stock market, you are buying a small slice of a company. When you invest in the bond market, you are essentially acting as a bank. Your investment is a loan that the borrower promises to pay back with interest.

Just like many folks get a mortgage to buy a house, bonds are loans to companies, or governments. There will be a set time period for the borrower to pay the original principal back, and there will also be an interest rate they pay back to the bond holders. A treasury bill is a loan to the U.S. government; it is stable because it is backed by the full faith and credit of the U.S. government. Many loans have collateral (assets, like a house is collateral for a mortgage) that are used to secure the loan. If a company couldn't pay back the loan, the assets would be used to pay back the bond holders. There are also state and municipal (local) bonds that can be used to build anything from roads to bridges to hospitals.

How many staircases should you have? You should have enough staircases to make you feel comfortable knowing you can't use the elevator in case of emergency. A great example of staircases coming into play is 2008. The global financial crisis came to a head in 2008. For some of us, this is a distant memory, but let me take you back. Lehman Brothers, a financial institution that survived for over 160 years, went bankrupt. Lehman collapsing was just the tip of the iceberg. Institutions were failing left and right. The S&P 500 (the temperature of the markets) was down 46% from October 2007 to March of 2009. If you had a million dollars in the S&P 500 in October of 2007, and looked at your account value in March of 2009, you would see your balance at $530,000. By then, the markets had witnessed Bear Stearns go bankrupt, and Bernie Madoff's fraud was revealed. The U.S. government started to bail out some of the largest financial institutions in the United States. If you had bought a house recently, say in 2007, you could owe more than your house was worth. The headlines just kept churning out more and more terrible financial news. You likely knew someone who had been laid off, or perhaps lost their house because they could no longer afford the payments.

The sense of impending financial doom seemed to be all around us. You want enough staircases so that when everything is at its worst and you look at your elevator—your million-dollar account that is roughly worth half that when the market is at its low point—you can say to yourself, I have my staircases; in the event of an emergency, I can access all the money I need, so I don't need my elevator right now. You leave your elevator alone, and your accounts stay invested. In fact, right after the market reached its lowest point in March 2009, it started to rebound. The S&P was up 60% (from its low point) just nine months later at the end of 2009. That same account value was still below one million dollars, but went back to one million dollars by 2013 (four years later). And if that money continued to remain invested, it was worth close to four million by the end of 2022.

This is the most important reason to have staircases or stabilizers—you have enough stabilizers so that you are able to leave those investments alone during turbulent times. Say you had decided you couldn't take your account value going down anymore, and took your money out of the market in March of 2009, your account would have a very different outcome.

The market often acts like a tennis ball, it bounces up just as quickly as it bounces down. But no one knows where the floor is—in other words, no one knows when the market is going to turn around and bounce back up. And if you take your money out at a low point, you have suffered tremendous losses, but then don't get the benefit of the bounce back up. You would have missed the 60% gain from March-December in 2009. You need enough staircases so that you feel OK when your elevator is having issues, and you won't touch it, because you will use the staircases until it is back up and running, so to speak.

3. **Why is TIME so important? And what can I do to maximize my TIME?**

You maximize your time by investing, rather than saving.

If you have a job, one of the most beneficial ways to start saving and investing for your future is through your employer sponsored retirement plan. I recognize, especially if you are young and relatively new to the workforce, retirement can seem eons away, and can be the last thing on your mind. But a key benefit of a retirement plan is that employers often match the money that you put into that account. For example, if you put in $100, your employer will contribute $100, and you've immediately doubled your money. I can't think of an easier way to double your money. Text me if you find an easier way!

Employers usually limit how much they match. They often state these limits as a percentage of your salary (for example, they may say they will match your contributions, up to 4% of your salary. Let's do the math on this: say you made $100,000 a year. If you decide to contribute $4000 a year (or 4% of your salary), your employer will put in another $4000. At the end of the year, you will have saved $8000.

Getting a $4000 match may not excite you terribly. But what does that match mean over your entire working career? Let's assume you worked forty years (from age twenty-five to sixty-five), and just to keep things simple, your salary didn't change for the entire forty years. At the end of those forty years, if you had continued to save 4% in your retirement plan each year, your employer will have contributed $160,000 to your retirement plan. That is your salary for over a year and half, that you received for essentially doing nothing, just because you decided to save for your future. That is the power of the match.

And that's not all. At the end of that forty years, assuming your money grows by 10% a year (which is the long-term average annual return of the stock market), you will have over 3.7 million dollars at age sixty-five. Not bad. And most experts recommend saving 10-15% of your salary each year for retirement. Including the match, this example was only saving 8% a year.

Let's look at the difference between investing your money, using a long-term strategy, versus putting your money somewhere "safe." If you invested that same money in the "safest" option in your plan, like a stable value fund (which is similar to a money market fund) and earned 2% every year, you would end up with just shy of $500,000 at the end of forty years. Or if you invested in bonds, with an annual return of 5% over the long-term, you would have just under 1 million dollars, a far smaller nest egg than 3.7 million.

Putting your money in "safe" places simply results in you having to overcome a different set of challenges when it comes to your finances. If you put your money in "safe" places, you will have to save more, and your money will grow at a much lower rate than if you invest in the market or other investments with higher rates of return. Essentially, you are making tradeoffs.

It's simple: 72/Rate of return = time for an investment to double.
When you are young and the amount you invest is fairly small, doubling your money won't seem like a huge difference, but the larger your nest egg becomes, the larger the impact of doubling your money. If you invest your money and earn an average of 10% every year, it will take 7.2 years for you to double your money. What if your return is lower than 10% a year? There is a formula that tells you exactly how long it will take you to double your money, it is called the rule of seventy-two.

The rule of seventy-two illustrates the impact of your annual rate of return. The lower your rate of return, the longer it will take for you to double your money. For example, if you had put your nest egg in a savings account that was earning 2% every year, it would take thirty-six years to double your money. Hopefully, I've convinced you from the rule of seventy-two and using a long-term, diversified approach to investing, seven years can make a huge difference in achieving financial independence.

Just a reminder: this is looking at very long-time horizons (decades). The market doesn't go up in a straight line, so this won't happen exactly every seven years with your account. Your account is more likely to go up and down in the short-term.

The amount of time you can invest can have a dramatic impact on your lifestyle.

Remember the example I shared at the beginning of the book: If you invested $10,000 at age twenty-one, assuming a 10% annual rate of return, you would have over $1.1 million dollars at age seventy-one. But if you waited just seven years, until age twenty-eight, you would have roughly half of that, a little over $600,000 at age seventy-one.

As your wealth increases, the impact of investing for seven more years increases as well. Let's say you wanted to stop working at some point and live off the money you've saved. If you want to ensure that you never run out of money, one strategy is to limit your withdrawals to 4% of your investment assets, so that you aren't depleting your nest egg.

If your nest egg is $2 million, according to the 4% rule, you will be able to take out $80,000 a year. Your monthly spending budget will be about $6700 (before taxes). Conversely, if you can delay using that money for a little over seven years and grow your nest egg to $4 million, using the 4% rule, you will be able to take out $160,000 a year, and your monthly spending budget will be about $13,300+ (before taxes). This can be a huge difference in your lifestyle.

An extra seven years can make a huge difference in your nest egg and lifestyle. This can go both ways: starting to invest earlier, or finding creative ways to create ongoing cash flow (real estate rentals/side hustles/part-time work) to delay taking money out of your accounts for a few years.

4. **Create your Investment Strategy**

You will have multiple goals in your financial vision. Your goals will likely include both short-term goals, that you would like to achieve in the next 2-3 years, and longer-term goals (like after your children leave the nest) that you aim to achieve in ten years, or even longer. A successful strategy aligns the time of your goal with the right type of investment. Consider the investments I highlighted as stabilizers for short-term goals. For longer-term goals, consider investing in the stock market, real estate, or starting a small business. One key advantage of entering the real estate rental market or investing in a profitable small business is ongoing cash flow. Cash flow can be very helpful when aiming for a budget surplus. Cash flow can help you achieve your financial visions now, with the opportunity of your investment growing in value over the long-term. The downside is that real estate rentals and small businesses require a significant investment of your time and relevant expertise. You will have to decide what works for you.

Does it make sense to get help?

Make no mistake, financial planning can be complex. You may be energized to achieve your vision and become financially independent, but recognize you need help with the technical aspects of Step 2. Let's spend some time talking about financial advisors. I get asked this next question a lot by women:

How can I find a financial advisor I can trust?

Financial Advisor, Certified Financial Planner®, Investment Advisor, Broker, all are different titles people trying to help you with your money call themselves. Struggling with how to find one you can trust? What do you do when you are trying to find a good doctor? Ask people you know. I would suggest asking people you know who are meticulous, likely to have spent time researching advisors. But don't just trust a friend's advice. Get a couple names from a couple different friends, meet with the advisors, and then ask yourself the following questions:

1. Did I feel comfortable with this person?
2. Did they listen to me?
3. Did I walk away from this conversation feeling more or less confused about my financial situation than before?
4. Did they offer to tell me how they get paid?

That sounds OK, but my real question is: how can I avoid being Bernie Madoffed? I heard that many of his clients were referred to him by their friends.

You have probably experienced a scam. They come in all sizes, big and small. We have all received emails from a "prince" asking for money, or a supposed phone call from the IRS. I'm not an expert on how to avoid all financial scams, but I do have specific actions you can take to avoid being the victim of a fraudulent advisor, like Bernie Madoff.

The steps below focus on fraudulent advisors and/or investments. I am not an expert in cybersecurity or online scams, so please note, the suggestions below do not cover online frauds. If you are concerned an advisor and/or an investment is a fraud, here are some situations to be wary about. I'm not suggesting each of these situations are a fraud, but I am suggesting that if you encounter any of the situations below, they could be warning signs for fraud. Act carefully, deliberately, and slowly.

First and foremost: **If it sounds too good to be true, it probably is**.

If someone is telling you their investment has never gone down in value (which is what Bernie told his clients) or "it's a sure thing" or that "you can double your money in six months," be very wary.

I'm not saying that there is no such thing as "get rich quick," but it really is the rare exception rather than the rule. Most wealthy people build their wealth over decades, not months. Your investments are not going to go straight up. If anyone ever shows you a chart that shows their investment always going up/never going down in value, be wary.

Often, Ponzi schemes are orchestrated as an "investment opportunity," not necessarily as a specific advisor. If a friend or acquaintance tries to sell you an "opportunity," ask if the investment is registered with the Securities and Exchange Commission (SEC). If it isn't registered, ask why. Not all investments have to be registered, but if you are considering an investment that isn't registered, be wary.

Avoid firms that demand secrecy. Secrecy can be appealing, but is a tool often used by scam artists. If someone tells you not to talk about an investment, that it is just open to a select few, be wary. Don't be afraid to ask questions! If the person offering you the investment seems in a rush or unwilling to address all of your concerns, be wary.

If you want to work with an advisor, first check if an advisor has had complaints by searching their name on FINRA's site: https://brokercheck.finra.org/

You may feel uncomfortable essentially questioning an advisor's credibility, especially one recommended by friends or family. You may think these extra steps are a waste of your time (after all, one of the reasons you are likely hiring an advisor is lack of time). But just remember the victims of financial fraud. Many of them lose everything. A best-case scenario is spending years fighting just for the chance at recapturing a fraction of your investment. It's worth it to spend a little time up front to expose any potential frauds.

Always ask these three questions to both prospective advisors or any advisor you are already working with:

1. **Are you a Certified Financial Planner (CFP®)?**

Can you work with someone that isn't a CFP® that you can trust? Absolutely; just recognize these are my suggestions for avoiding a scam advisor. Financial advisors are a relatively new profession, and don't have a single way to signal competency. Doctors and lawyers have educational requirements and must pass rigorous exams. Anyone with any education level and experience can call themselves a financial advisor. A Certified Financial Planner® must pass a rigorous exam as well as have several years of experience delivering financial planning. Even more importantly, CFP®s commit to high ethical standards. The CFP® designation isn't perfect but is the best certification in the industry when looking for someone with both competence and ethics.

2. **Does your firm work with a third-party custodian, and is there a way I can contact them to verify they are your custodian?**

If your advisor works for a very large, national firm, the chances that they are a fraudulent advisor are very low. However, many advisors want to be independent from large firms for various valid reasons and there are many excellent local financial planning firms.

A third-party custodian is a separate company that holds your assets and executes trades for your advisor (for example: buys and sells stocks for them). You can contact the third-party custodian to verify an advisor works with them. Examples of a third-party custodian could be Charles Schwab, Pershing, Bank of America, etc.

The way that Bernie Madoff and many other Ponzi advisors perpetuated their fraud is by producing fake documents, showing fake trades/account balances, etc. An advisor could never do that if they use a third-party custodian. I would never use an advisor unless they were part of a very large, national firm and/or used a third-party custodian.

3. **How do you get paid, and how much would I pay you in total dollars, not as a percentage of my assets, over the next twelve months? Is this a one-time fee or do I pay this fee annually?**

A big red flag is flying when an advisor says you are paying them no fees. Many who worked with Bernie Madoff thought they were getting a "great deal" because they weren't paying his firm a fee directly. Everyone has to make money in some way. No one is offering to manage your investments from the goodness of their heart. If an advisor or investment has no fees, be very wary. You should always know how and exactly how much your advisor gets paid.

Feel weird about asking these questions, especially if you already have an advisor? Blame me! Simply state: "I was reading this book about investing, and the author says it is irresponsible to not know how much you are paying your advisor in dollar amounts on an annual basis. I know we have gone over this before, but can you share it with me again?"

In addition to the fee you are paying your advisor, you are also likely paying investment management fees for any mutual fund, hedge fund or ETF (exchange traded fund) you own. A great question to ask an advisor is how they look at fees when choosing your investments. Does the advisor get a financial incentive for any products they sell?

Admittedly, this is a complicated question, as the advisor must manage multiple competing variables when managing investments. They will aim for the investments they select for you to have the highest possible return (appropriate for your investment objective) with the lowest possible fees. And they also will want to minimize your taxes (and selling an investment you own might be a very large taxable event). You may have an investment with higher-than-average fees, but the advisor may have a very good reason for keeping that investment. Having ongoing conversations with your advisor can help you better understand the reasons behind their recommendations.

A great thing to hear from an advisor is that they are a fiduciary, which simply means they are legally obligated to put your interests above their own. A fiduciary is no joke, as when you decide to be a fiduciary, your personal assets (your savings, home, etc.) are at risk if someone sues you professionally. Being a fiduciary is kind of like taking the Hippocratic oath.

Fiduciaries have strong personal incentives to act in your best interest. Now some big firms don't allow their advisors to be fiduciaries. Your advisor doesn't have to be a fiduciary to be a good advisor, but it certainly doesn't hurt. But a fiduciary isn't a panacea. Bernie Madoff called himself a fiduciary while clearly enacting principles opposite to that title.

How should I be paying my financial advisor?

The way investors pay advisors has evolved over time and is continuing to evolve. In the past, "stockbrokers" (a role that proceeded financial advisors) were paid a commission each time you bought and sold an investment. The commission was often a percentage of the amount that you bought or sold. This is very similar to the way real estate brokers are paid. Many advisors have moved away from that model and in recent years and "discount" brokerages have reduced commissions for trades to zero. I know I said to avoid "no fees"—please note that advice is for services an advisor provides to you. Zero/free trades are a legitimate way these firms are trying to get you to invest your money with their firm, and then get you to spend your money on other services (like hiring their advisors).

Why did advisors move away from commissions?

Advisors were paid only when their clients bought or sold something. An unintended consequence of the commission compensation model was that the more a client bought and sold investments, the more the stockbroker got paid, and their compensation wasn't impacted whether an investor made or lost money.

The industry evolved from stockbrokers (who typically only focused on investments) to advisors and now financial planners, who don't just provide advice on investments, but have expanded their scope to provide advice on a client's entire financial picture, including insurance, estate planning needs, budgets, taxes, etc.

Compensation evolved from commissions to "fee-based," which essentially means the advisor is paid a percentage of the assets they manage for you. A typical fee would be 1% of your assets annually, up to one million dollars. When managing assets north of a million, they will reduce their fee below 1%, typically on a sliding scale.

Many advisors say that fee-based compensation aligns their incentives with yours, when your assets increase, their compensation increases (and the reverse is true as well). But it's also important to understand how much you are paying your advisor each year, and ensure they are providing value for their fee, which can add up over time.

Let's look a hypothetical example. You are working with a fee-based advisor and they are managing $500,000 of your assets at a 1% annual fee. You would be paying them $5000 every year (or 1% of $500,000). You don't write a check for that amount, but in non-financial speak, rough $14 daily is skimmed off the top, before your daily balance is determined. It's painless, but less transparent than if you paid an advisor a check for their services every year.

An emerging way advisors are getting paid is a flat fee/fee for service model, similar to how you may pay an attorney (a hourly fee based on the work they do for you).

How much should I pay an advisor?
I wish there was an easy answer. As with most questions in finance, it depends. Two things that to consider are the complexity of your financial situation and the value your advisor provides.

What value does an advisor provide?
If you asked my questions above and found an advisor that you personally gelled with, they can be a fantastic resource to help you build and sustain wealth. There will be a mixture of quantifiable and less measurable ways an advisor provides value. Many financial decisions are interconnected and one decision you make can have a waterfall effect on several components of your finances. You don't know what you don't know. Many advisors have helped clients tremendously by avoiding costly mistakes that could have a massive impact over time.

Here are just a couple examples of the value a financial advisor can provide, though there are many more. An advisor may be able to help you reduce the fees you pay on your investments, which can add up to a huge sum of money for a long-term investment. Tax planning—not someone doing your taxes but creating a plan to help you minimize your taxes—can create significant savings that you will benefit from every year going forward. They can also help you prepare for or respond to life events (you just received an inheritance, you are not sure when you can retire, you don't know when to take Social Security). The cumulative impact of working with someone who understands the ever-changing environment, regulatory requirements and can develop a strategy to maximize your wealth can be extremely significant.

Just like any professional service, you could potentially do the work yourself, but it may take you longer and you may be making decisions without all the needed information, that could cost you later. You have to personally decide if you want to work with an advisor and decide what level of support is right for you. (i.e., unlimited access costs more, but may be worth it, depending on your specific needs).

Perhaps you aren't quite ready to work with an advisor, but are ready to start investing. There are products that don't help you with your financial plan, but can help you invest.

You can purchase the expertise of a professional investment manager by investing in a mutual fund or an ETF (exchange traded fund). 52% percent of American households own mutual funds.[xxvii] When you own a mutual fund or ETF, you become an owner of a very tiny part of a bunch of companies. These funds typically own hundreds of different companies. You buy shares of a specific fund (like the XYZ fund), and each share will include a tiny piece of ownership in all the companies the XYZ fund owns. If you own 100 shares of the XYZ fund, which is priced at $10 a share, then your account value is $1000. There is absolutely no risk that you will lose any of your shares. You are always going to have 100 shares, unless you decide to sell those shares, or buy more. But the value of those shares will go up and down. Just like prices for things you buy go up and down. Just like the value of your house goes up and down.

The fluctuation in price of the investments you own doesn't actually impact you unless you buy or sell your investments. In shorter time periods, your account value will go down. Personally, I've seen my accounts go down by 20 or 30% in a short period of time. In fact, it is fairly common to see the value of your shares go down during periods of market turmoil.

At the same time, the probability of you losing all your money is pretty low. In order for you to lose all your money, the hundreds of companies in XYZ fund would need to go bankrupt at the same time. And if all of the companies in a XYZ fund go bankrupt at the same time, likely the world itself is experiencing a much bigger catastrophe that will take your mind off the value of your investments. In other words, because these funds contain many different companies, they are diversified, and you are not risking putting all your money in one place. Buying a fund makes it easy to diversify, instead of buying hundreds of different individual stocks, you can purchase one fund.

Mutual funds and ETFs have many different flavors, you can own different size companies, or invest in certain industries. You can even invest in socially responsible or impact funds, perhaps a fund that only invests in companies trying to reduce climate change, for example.

Some funds are actively managed, meaning a portfolio manager actively decides which companies to invest in, and some are passively managed, which means the fund simply tries to mirror an index, i.e., invests in the exact same companies that are in an index (like the S&P 500 index). Actively managed funds are trying to outperform the index, but typically have higher fees than passively managed funds.

What is an index?

I've had many people (men and women) sheepishly tell me they hear terms like the Dow Jones, the S&P 500, and the NASDAQ, and don't really know what they are, so let's start there.

The Dow is just a list of thirty very large companies in the United States. When you hear the Dow has gone up or down, it simply means the collective change in share price of those thirty companies from the day before. (A share price is how much you would pay for one share of a company). The S&P 500 (the title gives you a hint) is a group of 500 U.S. companies. An index fund is an easy way to invest in all 500 companies at once (rather than purchasing shares in each company). These indices tend to be representative of how the market is doing at large, which is why they're used as common measurements.

Knowing your financial personality can help you avoid pitfalls on the path to financial independence. For those with an abundance mindset, creating your vision can provide the motivation to make changes in your spending habits, leading to a budget surplus. You can make an active tradeoff between getting closer to the life you want to lead vs. that thing you want to buy. For those with a scarcity mindset who may have the wealth to be financially independent, ask yourself, what is stopping you from achieving your vision?

Many women I've worked with have the STRESS financial personality. Consider actively choosing stabilizers that help you feel more secure. Then invest to grow wealth, rather than save out of fear. Time makes a huge difference in wealth creation. For those just starting out, your investment strategy can be as simple as investing in an index fund or ETF.

And for those who AVOID the topic of money and investing, perhaps working with a financial advisor is the best path for you to achieve financial independence. Whatever you do, start now.

CHAPTER 9: BREAKING THE MONEY TABOO FOR THE NEXT GENERATION

Simhasana

You can't take yourself too seriously when you do Lion's breath. After you take a deep inhale, and while doing a forceful exhale you stick your tongue out all the way and look up to the sky. It is a great way to release stress. Talking to kids about money doesn't always have to be a serious discussion. In fact, I urge you to not take yourself too seriously, which helps make this entire topic less intimidating for the next generation.

Your experiences in childhood helped shape your financial personality, including if you feel comfortable talking about money. These experiences include both big and small moments. You won't be able to control what specific memories influence your children or grandchildren. But what you can do, especially for your daughters and granddaughters, is to talk about money—not just in terms of what to buy and what not to buy—but to talk about investing with the next generation. Here are a couple of ideas to get you started.

A different type of birthday gift

Obviously, every child is different, but when your children and grandchildren start to write lists in anticipation of their birthday and you see a gift card on that list, instead of purchasing that gift card, open an investment account for them. You can use the money you would put toward a gift card and make an investment in the actual company they listed. Investing is easier than ever; many companies have little to no fees to get started.

The great news is that many firms now have apps that children can easily download to see their investment. Young people can experience the ups and downs that come with investing in the stock market. Just like anything, you want to make sure to have guardrails and regular check-ins with your child/grandchild. Set up check-ins twice a year (or at least on every birthday) to review what has happened with their investment and listen to how they have experienced their investment.

As you start to expose the next generation to investing, you will begin to see their financial personality come out fairly quickly. I have one niece who views money like a puzzle, and she immediately started researching other companies she could buy. I can tell she enjoys checking her investments on her app. Another niece is more avoidant of money, and has never downloaded the app. It's just not a priority to her. Knowing that, I keep encouraging her to check it out, and she recently shared she wants to sit down with me to learn more about it next time we get together. I'm careful not to judge either approach. My approach is to make investing, and talking more about investing, a familiar and normal conversation for both of them.

Frequently, parents share with me that one of their children is the "responsible" one and the other will spend like there is no tomorrow. Rather than compare and despair, use this knowledge to your advantage. My mother, knowing that I had an abundance mindset, used an incentive approach with me: If I reached certain academic goals, she would reward me with some purchase I wanted. It worked. If you want to encourage children with an abundance mindset to save, consider identifying a goal that is very motivating for them, and offering to match the amount they can save toward that goal.

Twelve topics you can share during those twice per year-check ins:
I think we've established that the jargon around investing can be overwhelming, and there aren't a lot of traditional avenues for the next generation to learn about investing. Take one topic per check-in and share it with your child or grandchild. These topics are geared toward teenagers

and young adults. The explanations below are starting points for each topic that you can utilize, my attempt to simplify complex concepts, not textbook definitions. Many financial experts will point out that I am not completely technically accurate or didn't provide you with all the information. But would you rather your doctor share what is going to happen in a way that you understand, or be so technically correct that you have no idea what they are saying?

Topic 1: What is a stock?

When you buy a stock, you are buying ownership in part of a company. Did you know that in a condo building, multiple people pool their resources so that each can own part of the building? The funding from the group makes the entire building possible. Companies allow people to buy stock, to own part of the company. The money from the stock allows the companies to invest and grow their business. Each company issues shares of stock. A share is like owning one apartment in a condo building. Companies sell lots of shares of stock. When you buy a share of a company, the price of the share goes up and down (just like condo prices go up and down). The stock market keeps track of all of the values of all of the shares for all the companies that have stock each day.

Topic 2: Are there different types of stocks?

Stocks are arranged in all sorts of categories. One category is all about the size of a company. You may see a company described as a large-cap or mid-cap or small-cap stock. A cap in this instance is not something you put on your head, it indicates the size of the company. Small-cap stocks are smaller companies that perhaps are just starting out. Large-cap stocks are really big, Fortune 500 companies such as Apple, Amazon, etc., and mid-cap stocks are somewhere in between.

Topic 3: What is diversification?

If you are a sports fan, you probably root for more than one team. Myself, the Chiefs, Royals, Kansas Jayhawks (Rock Chalk). The more teams you root for, the more chances you have to win. If you had invested all of your money in Blockbuster (you may have to explain what Blockbuster is to your kids, a fun exercise in its own right), you would be broke. If you invest in multiple companies and industries, the likelihood that all of them will go out of business at the same time is much lower.

Topic 4: What is a mutual fund?

Mutual funds remind me of chefs. Everyone can make dinner, but a money chef's professional role is to find the best ingredients, no matter what the season, and assemble the right ingredients in the right way to create an amazing menu. You pick the dish that is right for you.

The people who manage mutual funds are the chefs of the stock market. Their full-time job is to find the best companies to invest in, understand the current market conditions (i.e., season) and provide a menu of dishes (aka mutual funds). You can pick the mutual fund that is right for you.

Topic 5: What is the Dow, or the S&P 500?

The Dow is just a list of thirty very large companies in the United States. When you hear the Dow has gone up or down, it simply means the collective change in share price of those thirty companies from the day before. (A share price is how much you would pay for one share of a company). The S&P 500 (the title gives you a hint) is a group of 500 US companies. An index fund is an easy way to invest in all 500 companies at once (rather than purchasing shares in each company).

Topic 6: What is a financial goal?

Everything you want to achieve will cost money. Maybe you want to buy a car, a financial goal is your strategy to make and save enough money to pay for that car. Our family has multiple financial goals, we are (insert your goals here). We have a financial plan that keeps track of all our financial goals. For long-term goals that are five plus years away, we invest our money to make it work for us, i.e., grow, to help us meet our goals. One of the most important parts of our financial plan is our plan "B"—our emergency fund, which we can use when something doesn't go the way we planned, like our car breaking down.

Topic 7: What is a dividend?

Remember when we talked about owning stock is like owning a condo? Let's say your condo building earned some extra money by hosting parties in the common space. They give all residents a check, splitting the proceeds by percentage ownership. If you owned stock in a company and the company had a good year and made extra profits, sometimes companies decide to "give back" some of the proceeds from that good year to their shareholders in the form of a divided, which is a payment for every share that you own.

If you owned 100 shares and the company had a $.50 dividend, you would receive $50. Unless you say otherwise, that dividend payout is typically re-invested in the stock. In other words, the $50 that you receive would be used to buy you additional shares in the company. You do have the option to receive that dividend in cash, which is sometimes a strategy used by retirees to receive income but keep their original investment.

Topic 8: What is the difference between growth and value investing?

One way to explain these two terms is to compare the styles of two different investment managers (aka money chefs). A money chef focused on growth is most interested in investing in companies growing at a faster rate than before. Growth chefs are like music producers, they are trying to find that breakout star. A value chef is a little more boring. A value chef is interested in investing in a solid company, that for some reason or another has a stock price that is lower than the actual value of the company. Value investors are great bargain shoppers, just like my mother. My mother was very focused on the quality of the things she bought; cheap wasn't necessarily better, she wanted something to last, but she also wanted a good bargain. My mother was a fantastic value chef.

Topic 9: What are interest rates?

Simply put, interest rates are how much it will cost anyone to borrow money. Interest rates are controlled by the federal reserve, and their movements are closely followed and zealously reported on by the financial media because they are reliable, predictable news events. The federal reserve meets eight times per year. These meetings give the financial media at least three stories each time they meet.

Story 1: Will they raise/lower interest rates, and by how much?

Story 2. The impact of a potential raise/lowering of interest rates

Story 3. After the meeting: did they raise or lower rates?

This creates two dozen predictable, easy to write stories each year, so of course the financial media likes to cover the federal reserve, and as a result, you hear a lot of chatter about the impact of interest rates, as well as how to invest when interest rates go up or down.

But at the end of the day, interest rate changes are, by definition, short term events. The fed will meet in about another six weeks and things could change again. I'm not saying you should ignore interest rates. If you are buying or re-financing your house, interest rates should be a consideration. But as a long-term investor, the importance of interest rate changes is overstated, in my humble opinion.

Topic 10: What are bonds?

Just like many folks get a mortgage to buy a house, bonds are loans to companies, or governments. There will be a time period, say five years, for the borrower to pay the original amount of the loan (principal) back, and there will also be an interest rate they pay back to the bond holders. A treasury bill is a loan to the U.S. government; it is stable because it is backed by the full faith and credit of the U.S. government. Many loans have collateral (like a house is collateral for a mortgage) that is used to make the people lending the money feel comfortable that the borrower can pay back the loan. If a company couldn't pay back the loan, the collateral would be used to pay back the bond holders. There are also state and municipal (local) bonds that can be used to build anything from roads to bridges to hospitals.

Topic 11: What is the difference between a mutual fund and an IRA?
If you buy a candy bar, you get both the candy itself and the wrapper. What you are investing in, such as a mutual fund, or an individual stock (like the company Apple), or a high yield savings account, is the candy, and the type of your account is the wrapper. The options of what you can invest your money in–aka, the candy, are endless.

First, you should decide the type of account for your investment–aka, the wrapper. There are many different types of accounts. The type of account will designate who owns the account. For example, you could have an individual account, owned just by you, or a joint account, owned by you and someone else. In addition, the type of account can also designate how the money in the account can be spent. For example, IRAs (Individual Retirement Accounts), are designated specifically for retirement. They have certain tax advantages, but also restrictions on when you spend the money in the account. When you fund an IRA, you can't spend the money in the account until age 59 1/2 without a penalty. There are many other types of accounts that the government has created that have tax incentives. There are types or accounts specifically designed to save for college education (like 529s). They are multiple types of accounts designed to save for retirement—Individual Retirement Accounts, Roth IRAs, 401(k)s. There are even accounts to pay for health care costs, like HSAs (Heath Savings Accounts). Each of these different types of accounts have their own specific set of rules (how much you can contribute, who can contribute, what is not taxed vs. taxed, when you need to take money out).

Once you decide which type of account makes sense for you, then you decide what to invest in the account. You could open an IRA and invest that IRA into a mutual fund. An IRA is a type of account, a mutual fund is a professionally managed investment. A portfolio manager will be in charge of deciding what investments (individual stocks or bonds) are owned by that mutual fund.

Topic 12: What is the difference between an IRA and a Roth IRA?
As we shared before, IRAs are individual retirement accounts. A Roth IRA is just a specific type of IRA. The difference between the two is when you pay your taxes. Everyone must pay taxes. When you put money in an IRA, you typically get a tax-break that year, meaning you don't have to pay taxes on the money you put in the IRA. When you put money in a Roth IRA, you don't get a tax break when you put the money in, but you do get a tax break when you take the money out. If you are young, you have a long time until

retirement, and your investment has time to grow. It's usually a good idea to invest in a Roth IRA, because when you take the money out, you don't have to pay taxes on any money you put in, but you also don't have to pay taxes on the growth in your account.

For younger children, explain the "why" behind your financial decisions.

Breaking the money taboo with the next generation doesn't mean you have to talk about your net worth. Conversations about money don't have to be about numbers at all. Not sure how to start talking to children about money? Tell them what you are thinking!

OK, not everything that you are thinking, but the next time you make a relatively big purchase, talk to your children about the things you considered when making that decision. I'll give you an example. A few years ago, I bought a new car. And it was blue—I mean bright blue. My nephew was making fun of the color. There was a reason I made that decision, and it wasn't because I loved that bright blue color.

"Why do you think I bought a car that color?" I asked him.

Of course, he viewed the question with a little suspicion because I am "that" weird Aunt. I told him that I bought that bright blue car because I wanted to go to Belize. Of course, my answer confused him even more, and I started to share my decision-making process which led me to buying the above-mentioned blue beast. I told him that when I knew my previous car was on its last legs, I started a "new car" savings account. I had a specific amount automatically put into that account the day after each payday. I started researching cars and began to prioritize what features were important to me, and what wasn't important.

I have no need to go from zero to sixty anytime soon (after all, I live on an island where the highest speed limit is twenty-five mph) but I knew I would need 4WD or AWD to navigate the hills. Safety features are important to me, and I wanted enough room for my two dogs. After doing some research, I set a budget for my new car. Knowing that I have an abundance mindset, I gave myself an incentive for staying below my budget; I told myself that if I could purchase a car below my budget, any extra money would be "fun money."

Once I had saved up what I had decided to spend on the car, I went to a dealership and noticed a lot of bright blue models of the car I was looking at on the lot. I didn't really care what color my car was, so when the salesperson asked me what color I wanted, I asked, "Does the color I pick make any difference in price?"

The salesperson offered me a discount if I got the bright blue model, as they needed to make room for next year's inventory. The discount I got for my blue car took me under my budget and was enough to buy my plane ticket to Belize. My fun money made that trip happen!

What did my nephew learn from that story?

- Saving in advance for things you need helps you avoid debt.
- Prioritize what is important to you and know what is less important to you when making purchases.
- Decide how much you want to spend on something in advance.
- Negotiating can be as simple asking: "Does it make any difference in the price?"
- If you tend toward an abundance mindset, give yourself an incentive that helps you stay within budget. Make going under budget a reward, not a deprivation.

Anytime you are making a large purchase, talk through your thought process with your children or grandchildren. They can't read your mind, so could interpret your actions very differently than you intend them to without direct context from you. Help them understand all the considerations that go into a purchase, which helps them understand your values around money and how those values translate to real life situations.

The Million-dollar 35,000 gift.

I've spoken with many wealthy individuals over the years, and many are concerned about their children's success. They want their children to become financially independent on their own. They are concerned that the next generation might just be waiting for an inheritance, or they don't want to "spoil" the next generation. But at the same time, the safety nets that are available to you (like Social Security or a pension) may not be available to your children and grandchildren. There is a middle path where you can teach your children and grandchildren the value of hard work, but also fund a safety net that isn't outrageous.

The rule of seventy-two illustrates how time can be such a beneficial factor when it comes to investing. Under perfect circumstances, the best time to invest is when you are born. If you want to create a safety net for future generations, with a relatively modest initial investment, consider over-funding your children or grandchildren's 529 college savings account.

Starting in 2024, the government allows tax-free rollovers of up to $35,000 (lifetime limit) to Roth IRAs from a 529 plan. The rollover can only begin if the money has been in a 529 account for at least fifteen years. Let's look at a scenario:

You contribute $35,000 to your child's 529 plan the year they are born. This money would be above and beyond any savings you would set aside for their education costs. At age sixteen, if your child gets a job and has earned income over $6500, you can roll over $6500 (the current annual contribution limit for Roth IRAs) from the 529 to a Roth IRA in your child's name that year. Below lists how much you could roll over from the 529 to a Roth IRA each year until you hit the $35,000 lifetime limit, assuming the child had earned income equal/above the amounts for each year listed below.

Age	Amount from 529 rolled over into Roth IRA
16	$6500
17	$6500
18	$6500
19	$6500
20	$6500
21	$2500

The last year you roll over money from the 529 to the Roth IRA is when your child turns 21, rolling over $2500 to max out the $35,000 lifetime limit you can roll over from the 529 plan. That money will grow tax-free in your child's account. Assuming a 10% annual rate of return, your child will have over one million dollars in that Roth IRA when they reach age sixty. That is assuming they make zero additional contributions to the Roth IRA.

Roth IRAs also allow for a tax-free withdrawal of principal, which includes the $35,000 you originally contributed, after that money has spent five years in the Roth IRA. This means that at age twenty-six, your child would be able to access that $35,000 in case of an emergency without paying taxes or penalties. What a great way for the next generation to learn the impact of time on an investment. Time is on your side when it comes to investing.

CHAPTER 10: STARTING A NEW RELATIONSHIP WITH MONEY

Savasana

At the end of every class, we lie down and close our eyes for savasana, or corpse pose. Savasana marks the death of who we were at the beginning of class. Every class changes me in some small way, and I strive to take what I learned on the mat off the mat.

I met a guy who had a wedding ring with a skull on it. The skull was smooth like it had been in the bottom of a river for a thousand years, the water shaping the metal with gentle slopes instead of jagged edges. The skull was there to remind him that today could be his last day. Every time someone says something like that to me—"Carpe Diem," "you could die tomorrow!" or "live every day like it's your last"—I find it a little unfathomable. I understand their intention behind the sentiment, but if I lived every day like it was my last, why would I save anything, build anything, why would anyone ever have kids, get married, or plan anything? A more palatable idea to me is living every day like it is your first day in a strange place. I love to travel, and the first day I experience a new place, I seem to marvel at everything, because I'm seeing everything for the first time.

I recently had a week of travel. My schedule was pretty full: work, travel, speech, travel, rinse, repeat. One day on the road in south Florida, I had about an hour before I needed to go to the airport. On my way there, I realized my GPS sent me up a small road along the coast instead of the highway because there was an accident. I was getting closer to the airport and kind of dreading spending time there, and I kept seeing these little side streets to my right that led directly to the beach.

The planner in me told me to go straight the airport, but I flashed back to when I was a kid, when my dad (Charlie) would just impetuously pull over on the highway, because he saw a history sign or something that interested him. I decided to pull a "Charlie" and squeal onto one of the side streets (the squealing is a slight exaggeration).

I stopped the car, parked, and suddenly I was on the boardwalk and could see the ocean. An older woman with two young boys was just ahead of me. Mind you, I was wearing a black business suit and sand was getting in my work shoes. I paused to take off my blazer and my shoes and this little boy, probably six or so, just turned to me and gave me the tiniest little flower. It was perfect, no bigger than the tip of my pinkie, with a yellow center and white petals. He smiled at me, and I smiled back. Then I walked into the sand, fully realizing how silly I probably looked, but who cares?

The water was only another thirty or so feet away, so I climbed down a small dune, my feet feeling the warm, foamy sensation of home. I always feel like I have come home when I get in the ocean. My whole body just relaxed as I looked across the horizon, seeing the amazing blue green frothy being as if for the first time. And then I thought to myself, *this is how a business trip (or any day) gets infinitely better!* I lingered for about five or ten minutes, took a couple pictures, felt my feet getting buried by the water and the sand. I chuckled to myself, realizing the small "Charlie" I pulled made that day suddenly a thousand times better.

The journey to achieving your vision is where the magic happens. Don't miss that journey by anticipating the destination. Time and time again you hear stories of Olympic athletes feeling a sense of disappointment after they reach their goal. Because what is next? I think that is a key issue with retirement—what are your goals after you retire? Why not focus on your life right now, and find ways to enjoy the journey to its fullest?

I recognize this book is a whole practical menagerie of planning. I am pragmatic to the core, but this practice of getting more comfortable with finances isn't just about money. It's about intentionally creating the life you want. Now, not some time in the future. And most importantly, being present and open to this life. I've stopped spending my life anticipating future events and opened myself up to the joy of today.

And it all started with this very pragmatic thing that seemed to rule my choices and my life—money. Once I realized how I personally related to money, I gradually let go of all the beliefs and ideas I had held on to so tightly for so long. I stopped having to spend as an expression of my self-worth, which helped me become financially independent and have the life that I want now.

If you want to change your relationship with money, discovering your financial personality is the starting point. You can only change your unconscious beliefs by first becoming aware of your beliefs, and then letting the beliefs that no longer serve you go. Then, identify your financial vision: **Why are you saving and investing?** Please don't stress out over the exercise of creating your vision. You can't get it wrong, because it will change over time. The most important thing you can do for your future is to define what you want your life to look like, and what you view as your purpose – using what you have to help others.

Once you have created your vision, create your strategy to achieve your vision and become financially independent. You may view money like a puzzle and are excited to tackle your strategy head on. Or perhaps you view your finances as one big red pulsing ball of stress, and you decide to work with a financial advisor to help you create that strategy.

Finally, once you have created your strategy, you do the work. Being aware of your financial choices, and making intentional choices that move you closer to your vision is a daily practice. Some days you will do better than others. Be gentle with yourself. Use the things you have learned about yourself, and your relationship with money as opportunities to make changes.

And don't take anything, even gasp, money, too seriously. Recognize that the journey is the fun part. The first time I spoke to a group of people as a keynote speaker, knowing full well I had no idea what I was doing, I was terrified. Uncomfortable doesn't even begin to describe what I felt. But I took a few deep breaths. And I decided to get up on that stage, despite my discomfort. And after I finished my first talk, I knew a million things I could have done differently, but I was exhilarated. I hope your journey to changing your relationship with money, defining your vision and purpose leaves you feeling just as exhilarated.

ABOUT THE AUTHOR

Jean is a Certified Financial Planner® and an expert on financial personalities. Jean grew up as a spender in a family of savers, and found herself in thousands of dollars in credit card debt in her early 20s. But Jean changed her own relationship with money to become an intentional spender, and purposefully made financial choices to create the life that she wants - which includes multiple sources of income and a beautiful home in the Virgin Islands.

Notes

[i] The American Psychological Association, *Stress in America*™ survey, March 2022.
[ii] UBS, *Own Your Worth*, 2021.
[iii] Joyce W. Warren, *Women, Money, and the Law: Nineteenth-Century Fiction, Gender, and the Courts*, 2005.
[iv] Alice Kessler-Harris, *Women Have Always Worked, A Concise History*, 2018.
[v] James Royal Ph.D. and Arielle O'Shea "What is the Average Stock Market Return?" *NerdWallet*, May 2023.
[vi] Luca Pacioli, *Summa de Arithmetica*, 1494.
[vii] Andrew Barry, "Warren Buffet Has Amassed Over 90% of His Wealth Since He Turned 65," *Barron's,* March 2022.
[viii] Source: Vanguard Survey, 2020.
[ix] Source: Fidelity *Women and Investing Study*, 2021.

[x] Brad Barber and Terrance Odean, "Boys Will Be Boys: Gender, Overconfidence, and Common Stock Investment," *The Quarterly Journal of Economics*, Volume 116, Issue 1, February 2001, Pages 261–292.

[xi] Steven Garmhausen, "Women Make Great Financial Advisors, So Why Aren't There More?" *Barron's*, 2019.
[xii] The Nationwide Retirement Institute, *2022 Social Security Survey*, 2022.
[xiii] Adrian F. Ward and John G Lynch, Jr. "On a Need-to Know-Basis: How the Distribution of Responsibility Between Couples Shapes Financial Literacy and Financial Outcomes" *Journal of Consumer Research*, Volume 45, Issue 5, February 2019.
[xiv] Source: ssa.gov
[xv] "The History of the Pension Plan," due.com
[xvi] National Vital Statistics Reports, Vol. 54, No 14, April 2006.
[xvii] Source, World Bank.
[xviii] Source: U.S. Census, 2020.
[xix] Source: cdc.gov
[xx] Gabriella & Brian Bosche', *The Purpose Factor: Extreme Clarity for Why You're Here and What to Do About It*, 2022.
[xxi] Adam Grant, *Give and Take: A Revolutionary Approach to Success*
[xxii] Patrick L. Hill, Nicholas A. Turiano, Daniel K. Mroczek, Anthony L. Burrow, "The value of a purposeful life: Sense of purpose predicts greater income and net worth" *Journal of Research in Personality*, Volume 65, December 2016.
[xxiii] Richard H. Thaler, *Misbehaving: The Making of Behavioral Economics*, 2015.

xxiv Daniel Kahneman, Jack L. Knetsch, Richard H. Thaler, "Anomalies: The Endowment Effect, Loss Aversion and the Status Quo Bias. *Journal of Economic Perspectives*, 1991.

xxv Source: "Great Depression Facts," FDR Presidential Library & Museum.

xxvi Source: St. Louis Federal Reserve.

xxvii Investment Company Institute, "*Share of households owning mutual funds in the United States from 1980 to 2022*", 2022.

Made in the USA
Middletown, DE
07 December 2023

44868522R00106